JAZZ IMPROVISATION

FOR ASPIRING STUDIO MUSICIANS

(In 19 Sessions)

BY

MICHAEL G. CUNNINGHAM

DIGITAL INPUT AND FORMATTING BY

ADAM BOLL

i

AuthorHouse™ LLC
1663 Liberty Drive
Bloomington, IN 47403
www.authorhouse.com
Phone: 1-800-839-8640

Published by AuthorHouse 01/29/2014

ISBN: 978-1-4918-5977-3 (sc)
ISBN: 978-1-4918-5978-0 (e)

Library of Congress Control Number: 2014902014

Preface

There are a number of books available on this subject, and it is the hope of the author that this one will differ substantially. This book came about after about 20 years of trial and error and experimentation with willing students.

Who is this book for? Probably not for gifted jazz improvisers, because they frequently operate intuitively and do not evaluate and rationalize what they do. Many do not even read music. More power to them! However, when it comes to students who want to learn, they seem to fall in two categories. Some prefer a generalized intuitive approach, while others (aimed at in this book) want more rational involvement. So this book is primarily for aspiring studio musicians, and others who wish to know more about an elusive skill. This book tries for a balance between the creative and the rational part of the brain.

However, in a way, these sessions might also be useful for skilled practitioners who wish to renew and sharpen their skills. It is possible for improvisers to feel they are in a rut, and in need of different approaches.

These learning sessions require and come to life when there is a pianist/accompanist involved. While the student plays each step, either the teacher or another student should accompany at the piano. The basic learning unit is the eight-measure phrase, here called a strophe. And always each step requires an assiduous steady beat. The accompanist addenda in the back of the book make that process relatively simple. The addenda also help to clear up any questions concerning chordal symbols. The accompanimental chords are purposefully rhythmically basic, so that only the primary improviser will be rhythmically challenged. However, the accompanist may also play the given chords in an improvised rhythmic manner.

The first block of seven sessions establishes a routine of track presentation. Later sessions deal with various skills in a minimally logical order. The first block of nine sessions start off with pure sight-reading, and acquaintance with the two basic forms: Bifid (ABAC) and Ballad (AABA). Each of these is given in rhythms that are not too basic, nor too elaborate, and would be typical and appropriate for the initial statement of a melody that would be the basis for succeeding variation.

-M.G.C.

TABLE OF CONTENTS

Introduction

The various steps of a session can, and maybe should be rehearsed before presentation during the formal teacher-directed meeting. Indeed, nothing would be wrong with writing out responses ahead of time and playing them from memory during the lesson. However, in time the ideal response is entirely improvised.

Bifid forms have four strophes, each eight measures long, and in the following form: ABAC. Each of these letters represents an eight-measure strophe. A repeated letter signifies that a strophe is either repeated exactly or in slight variation. Notice how the Bifid form starts the same halfway through. Ultimately, during the "heat" of jazz improvisation, we will be dealing with constant melodic exploration, and it will be only the harmony that is repeated at the halfway point. In the Ballad form (AABA) the B strophe is the bridge or release. During the so-called Golden Era of American Popular Song (Kern to Arlen), this was the most popular form.

HARMONY: Roman numerals are used for spelling practice and to show how all keys are alike. As is demonstrated in the accompanist's addendum, any major-minor seventh chords usually have an added 9th. Also, any plain major triads, shown as capitol Roman numerals, usually have a 6th above the bass (and not first inversion). That is nothing new. However, there is a slight newness when dealing with Roman numerals. Those are mostly the same as one would find in traditional theory instruction, except that when a II^6 is encountered here, it does not mean first inversion, but rather a major triad with an added 6 above the bass. The same is true for IV. In that sense, there is no traditional nomenclature here for inverted chords because usually none is needed. And while the traditional Roman numerals for six or seven of the diatonic scale degrees are used, as in traditional theory lessons, here there are also diamond chord symbols for other chromatic levels.

RADICALLY NEW: Diamond levels and keys are figured chromatically from the tonic. The tonic is Diamond zero, Diamond 1 is a half-step above the tonic, Diamond 3 is three half steps above the tonic, and so on. A half-step under the tonic is Diamond 11. The only diamond levels that will be indicated are 1, 3, 6, 8, 10, and 11. (In flexible typing systems, a number could be placed within the shape of a diamond to more efficiently imply diamond levels and chords.)

The harmony in this book is somewhat basic, and the progressions are deliberately functional (ii – V – I) and it is wise to keep that so. While after 1960 there was much harmonic experimentation, and proclamations of a metamorphosis into a new, more enlightened harmony, even radically isolated cases of so-called atonal jazz, the reality is that most of it seemed to lead nowhere, while severely diminishing audience appeal. (A case of self-destructiveness?) Often accompanimental chords and progressions became so distorted and obscured that only the improviser could relate to it, and maybe not even then. An ideal example would be substitute chords gone awry. Jazz has always relied on substitute chords, but just how far off and distorted should those chords be Considering how far this practice was taken after 1960, perhaps moderation is in order a half-century later. Without moderation, the accompanying harmony could merely seem to transpire along with the soloist without any sort of heard harmonic relationship. There were even frequent attempts, especially in arranging, to create a non-functional harmony where chords succeed one another in no particular relationship: arbitrary chordal structures in an arbitrary order. Any kind of concocted music will attract a fringe audience for a while, and it may temporarily seem fresh and original. We, however, will concern ourselves with reaching the biggest possible audience, using an ideal jazz tonal language. We want to reach out and connect with a larger constituency than presently supports jazz.

Certain later exercises in the book alternate between "plain" and "rarified." It is the progression of the chords that make them plain or rare. To classify something here as "plain" is not to imply inferiority. It merely implies that the harmony of many Golden Era songs move that way, and improvisation is somewhat easier. On the other hand, the "rare" type demands closer attention during improvisation. There is some degree of unpredictability. Rarified harmony might well stay in chords for longer periods than plain harmony. However, rare chordal harmonic plans in subtle ways still relate to ii – V – I functional harmony. All feasible harmonic plans still very subtly enhance the tonic chord through planned root movement. So, never believe that rare means non-functional harmony.

In the same vein of reaching the largest possible audience, sequence exercises are emphasized. Picture a melodic idea or pattern as an information bit. All too often jazz performers unwittingly load their solos with too much information. While there also seems to be an audience for this type of improvisation, it is all too small. There must be a lowering of information by having "bits" return, and the sequence exercises in this book get the student thinking in that dimension. Like all techniques, it could conceivably be overused, but the exercises here help the student in moving in that direction.

RHYTHM: As was suggested in the preface, the rhythms presented in the two opening sight reading pieces at the beginnings of the first nine sessions are deliberatively restrained, as illustrative of the rhythmic approach to stating basic tunes before any jazz melodic variation begins.

Perhaps the basic improvisatory rhythmic movement is in eighth notes. And it is not true that a swing approach to 8ths is always appropriate. In fact, in studying the recordings of the greatest jazz figures of the 1950s and 60s, one hears an unpredictable alternation between swing and straight 8ths.

For students who don't fully understand swing rhythms, the following is an illustration. In swing rhythm, the top stave is played and rhythmically transposed to sound like the second stave.

During the many arpeggiation exercises, a swing feel may indeed be used, if feasible.

An added note: A jazz musician can only be called such if he or she is able to play classic traditional jazz melodies (Golden Era jazz favorites) from memory. This is the heart of the whole movement. Without this skill, the player is merely dabbling in mannerisms.

SESSION 1
Skill A: Reading swing rhythms.

A.1) In a steady tempo, read through the following bifid-form. Bifids repeat the opening few measures in the 17th measure, and could be described as an ABAC form.

SESSION 1 Bifid

(Accompanist No. 1)

A.2) In a steady tempo, read through the following ballad-form. Ballad forms repeat the opening few measures in the 9th and 25th measures, and could be described as an AABA form. The B section is the Release/Bridge.

SESSION 1 Ballad

(No. 2)

Skill B: Arpeggiation in plain and rare harmonic progressions.

B.1) Plain: Arpeggiate in straight 8th notes.

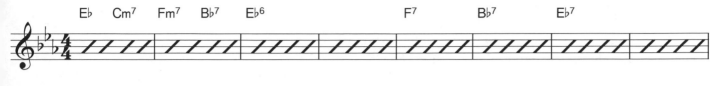

(No. 3)

B.2) Rare: Arpeggiate similarly, even though each chord lasts two measures.

(No. 4)

Skill C: Repeating a pattern.

Repeat the given short pattern in every measure, staying within the given dyads. The third note should always be a chromatic lower neighboring tone. When there are two dyads per measure, accommodate them as best you can. The last note of the pattern is changeable to smooth out getting to the next level.

Fig. 5

C.1) An opening strophe.

(No. 5)

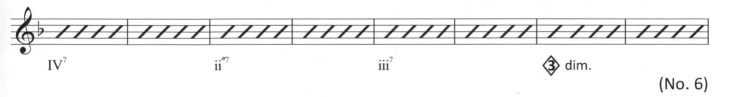

(No. 6)

5

Skill D: Sequencing.

To sequence is to repeat an idea at another pitch level. If the chord repeats in the next measure, then the repeat is at a higher or lower level in that chord.

D.1) Short sequence: The following is an opening strophe. In the blank measures, sequence what was in the previous two while staying within the indicated chords.

Sequence

Sequence

(No. 7)

D.2) Longer sequence: The following is also an opening strophe. Sequence whatever took place in the opening four measures, while staying in the indicated chords.

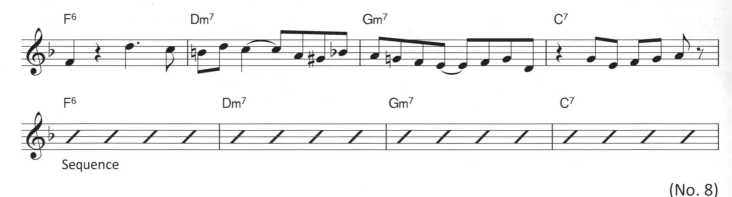

Sequence

(No. 8)

Skill E: Tag ending formulas - The Trice Formula.

Sometimes the last melodic idea in a song can be repeated three times to give a sense of satisfying closure. In doing so, you must postpone the last note of the melody until the very end.

Here are the ends of two songs. A variation of this trice-formula is to sequence the second time up to a higher key, and the third time back to the home key. Demonstrate this formula on both endings.

SESSION 2
Skill A: Reading swing rhythms.

A.1) In a steady tempo, read through the following bifid-form.

SESSION 2 Bifid

(No. 9)

A.2) Read through the following ballad-form.

SESSION 2 Ballad

(No. 10)

Skill B: Arpeggiation in plain and rare chordal progressions.

B.1) Plain: Arpeggiate in straight 8th notes.

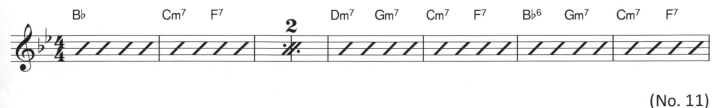

(No. 11)

B.2) Rare: Arpeggiate similarly.

(No. 12)

Skill C: Repeating a pattern.

Notice that this pattern occupies two measures, and of course must relate to changing chords.

Fig. 14

C.1) Opening strophe: Stay in the given dyads.

(No. 13)

C.2) Opening strophe:

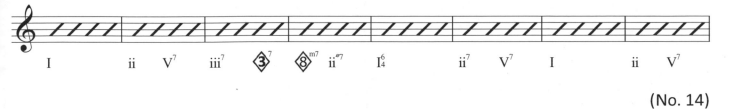

(No. 14)

9

Skill D: Sequencing.

D.1) An opening strophe: In the blank measures, sequence what was in the previous two, being careful to relate to the given chords.

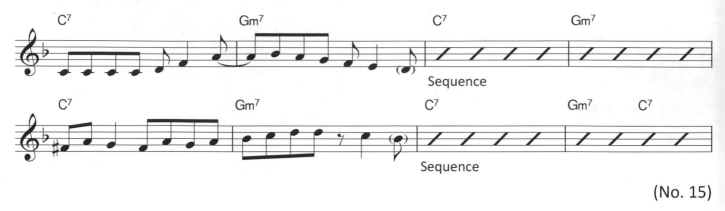

(No. 15)

D.2) An opening strophe: Do a 4-measure sequence.

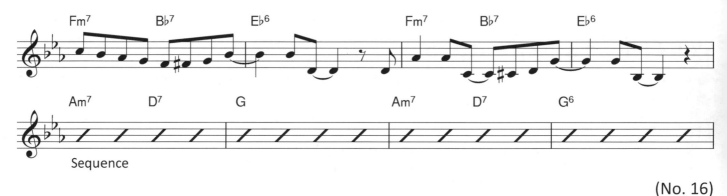

(No. 16)

Skill E: Tag ending formulas - The Deceptive Cadence (vi).

E.1) Finish the last few measures of a hypothetical song, and on the very last melodic note, give a vi chord instead of a I chord. Then repeat the same ending and end on a I chord. Here are a couple sample endings on which to practice (E.1 and E.2).

SESSION 3
Skill A: Reading swing rhythms.

A.1) Read through the following bifid-form.

SESSION 3 Bifid

(No. 17)

A.2) Read through the following ballad.

SESSION 3 Ballad

(No. 18)

Skill B: Arpeggiation in plain and rare chordal progressions.

B.1) Plain: Arpeggiate in straight 8th notes.

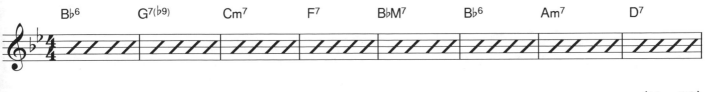

(No. 19)

B.2) Rare: Arpeggiate similarly.

(No. 20)

Skill C: Repeating a pattern.

C.1) Opening strophe: Stay in the given dyads.

(No. 21)

C.2) Opening strophe in chord symbols.

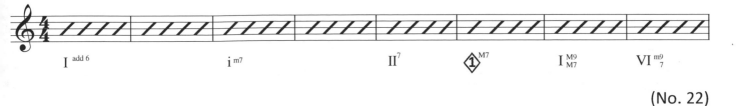

(No. 22)

13

Skill D: Sequencing.

D.1) Two measures length: Repeat the idea at another pitch level, while staying in the given chords.

(No. 23)

D.2) Four measures length: Do similarly.

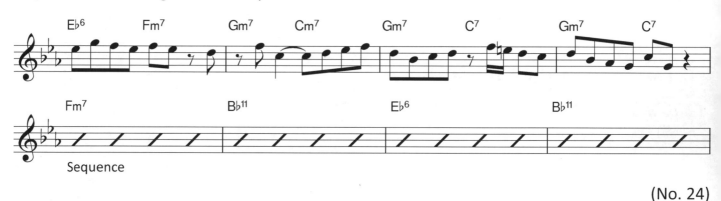

(No. 24)

Skill E: Tag ending formulas - The Deceptive Cadence (vi).

Sometimes the previous two ending formulas can be combined with a dominant pedalpoint in the bass during the last four or eight measures of the song proper as well as extended tag measures. Try it with two different endings (E.1 and E.2). At the asterisks, you can choose either an abrupt ending, or a retard with a final note fermata.

E.1

E.2

SESSION 4
Skill A: Reading swing rhythms.

A.1) Read through the following bifid.

SESSION 4 Bifid

(No. 25)

A.2) Read through the following ballad. (Model: "Autumn Nocturne.")

SESSION 4 Ballad

(No. 26)

Skill B: Arpeggiation.

B.1) Plain: Arpeggiate in straight 8th notes.

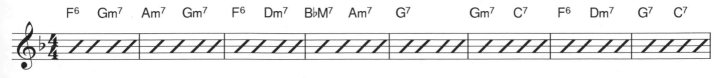

(No. 27)

B.2) Rare: Arpeggiate similarly.

(No. 28)

Skill C: Repeating a pattern.

Here, the last four notes are to be a variable connective to the next measure.

C.1) Opening strophe: Stay in the given chords.

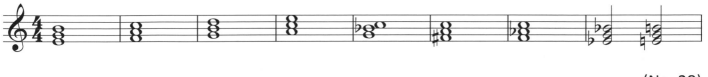

(No. 29)

C.2) An opening strophe in chord symbols.

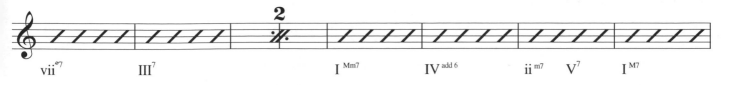

(No. 30)

Skill D: Sequences.

D.1) An opening strophe: Measures 3 and 4 should have a response idea, rather than a sequence. Measures 7 and 8 should have a sequence of 5 and 6. You must relate to the given chord symbols.

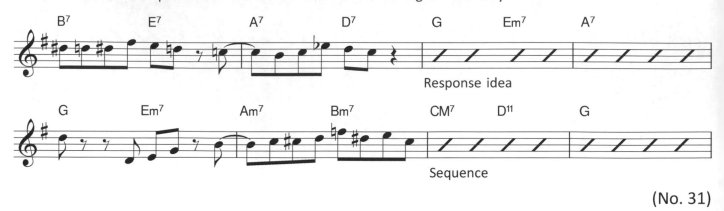

(No. 31)

D.2) An opening strophe: Sequence the opening four measures.

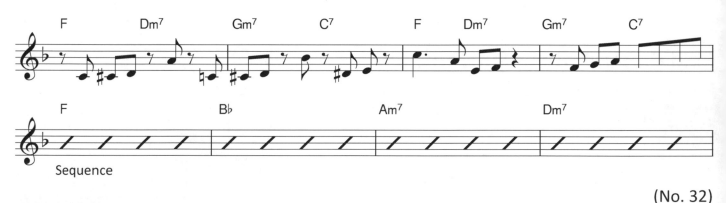

(No. 32)

Skill E: Tag ending formulas.

Sometimes, when the last chord is reached, an extended short coda can feature a tonic pedalpoint, with perhaps such a chord progression as I --- diamond 3 --- II --- diamond I --- Tonic.

E.1) Try it with the following two endings.

⬧③   II^7 ⬧①^{m7} I

Supplemental Information:

The OCTATONIC SCALE consists of eight different pitches in the pattern, whole tone - half tone - whole tone - half tone, etc. up to the octave. In Classic Mainstream Jazz it seems to be used in two ways: 1) When one wishes to be oblique for a while - not sounding as if you are in any key, and 2) On any major-minor seventh chord starting on the 3rd of the chord and ascending, beginning with a whole tone.

W   H   W   H etc.

SESSION 5
Skill A: Reading swing rhythms.

A.1) Read through the following bifid.

SESSION 5 Bifid

(No. 33)

A.2) Read through the following ballad.

SESSION 5 Ballad

(No. 34)

Skill B: Arpeggiation in plain and rare chordal progressions.

B.1) Plain: Arpeggiate in straight (non-swing) 8th notes.

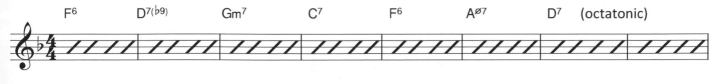

(No. 35)

B.2) Rare: Arpeggiate similarly.

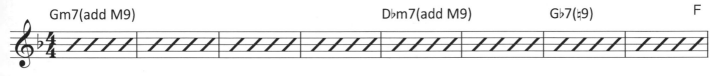

(No. 36)

Skill C: Repeating a pattern.

C.1) An opening strophe: Stay in the given chords.

(No. 37)

C.2) An opening strophe in chord symbols.

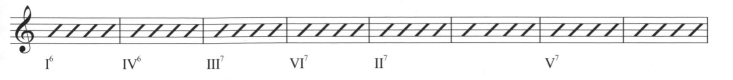

(No. 38)

Skill D: Sequences.

D.1) Here is an opening strophe: Measures 3 and 4 should have a response idea, rather than a sequence. Measures 7 and 8 should sequence 5 and 6. You must relate to the given chord symbols.

Response idea

Sequence

(No. 39)

D.2) Here is the opening strophe: Sequence the opening four measures.

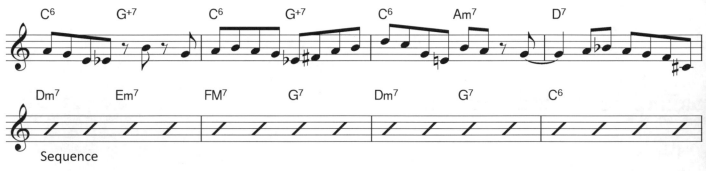

Sequence

(No. 40)

Skill E: Tag ending formulas.

Sometimes there can be extended measures on the end of a song involving the following chord progression, roots dropping by 5ths to the Tonic chord. You begin this progression when you have reached the final note of the song proper.

iii7 (or iii half-diminished 7) to VI to ii to V to I. Try it with the following two endings (E.1 and E.2).

E.1   iii etc.

E.2   iii etc.

Supplemental Information:

Some famous Jazz Repertory songs have unusual forms. "Night and Day" is a long Bar form (AAB). "I'll Remember April," "Old Devil Moon," and "You Are the Sunshine of My Life" have true Ternary forms (ABA). On your own, try to figure out the form of "Bluesette."

22

SESSION 6
Skill A: Reading swing rhythms.

A.1) Read through the following bifid.

SESSION 6 Bifid

(No. 41)

A.2) Read through the following ballad.

SESSION 6 Ballad

(No. 42)

Skill B: Arpeggiation in plain and rare chordal progressions.

B.1) Plain: Arpeggiate in straight 8th notes.

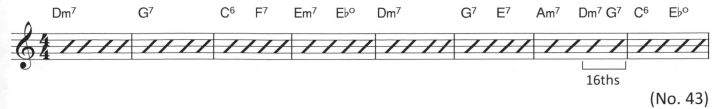

(No. 43)

B.2) Rare: Arpeggiate similarly.

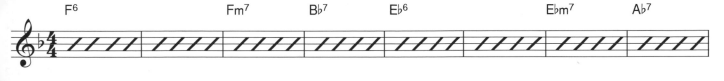

(No. 44)

Skill C: Repeating a pattern.

C.1) An opening strophe.

(No. 45)

C.2) An opening strophe.

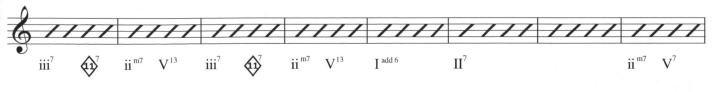

(No. 46)

Skill D: Sequences.

D.1) An opening strophe. Measures 3 and 4 should sequence 1 and 2. Likewise, measures 7 and 8 should have a sequence of 5 and 6. You must relate to the given chord symbols.

Sequence

Sequence

(No. 47)

D.2) An opening strophe. Sequence the opening four measures.

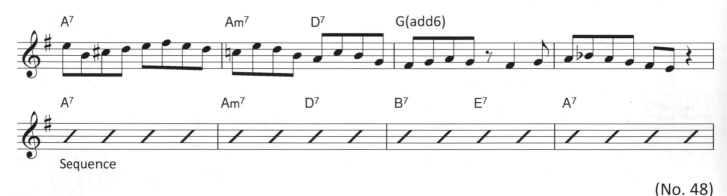

Sequence

(No. 48)

Skill E: Tag ending formulas.

When you reach the last note of the melody proper, the bass can descend chromatically from the tritone. Expressed in chord symbols, the bass line in half notes would be:

Diamond 6 half-dim. --- iv m7 --- iii m7 --- diamond 3 dim.7 --- ii m7 --- diamond 1 M7 --- I. Try it with E.1 and E.2.

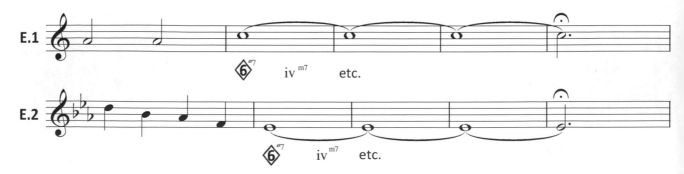

Supplemental Information:

In slow music, a spastic/rubato improvised line can be very effective while accompanied by a steady beat of chord changes. Try doing that with the first strophe of a famous memorized song.

SESSION 7
Skill A: Reading swing rhythms.

A.1) Read through the following bifid.

SESSION 7 Bifid

(No. 49)

A.2) Read through the following ballad.

SESSION 7 Ballad

(No. 50)

Skill B: Arpeggiation in plain and rare chordal progressions.

B.1) Plain: Arpeggiate in straight (non-swing) 8th notes.

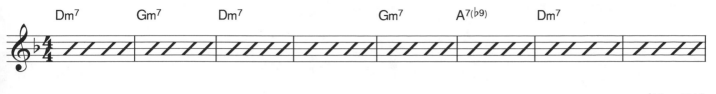

(No. 51)

B.2) Rare: Arpeggiate similarly.

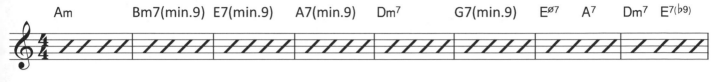

(No. 52)

Skill C: Repeating a pattern.

C.1) An opening strophe. Clearly relate to the given chords.

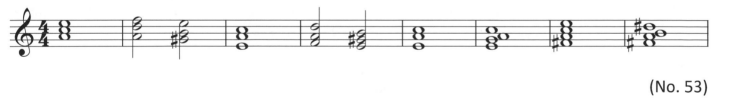

(No. 53)

C.2) An opening strophe in chord symbols.

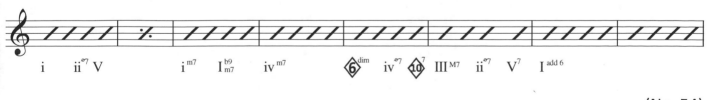

(No. 54)

Skill D: Sequences and Responses.

D.1) Here is an opening strophe. Measures 3 and 4 should respond to 1 and 2. Measures 7 and 8 should have a sequence of 5 and 6. You must relate to the given chord symbols.

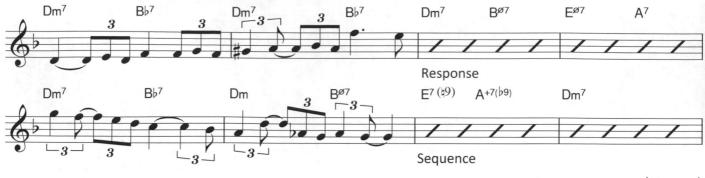

(No. 55)

D.2) An opening strophe. Sequence the opening four measures.

Sequence (Same Harmony)

(No. 56)

Skill E: Tag ending formulas.

Here is the harmonic plan involving chordal Roots that drop by a Perfect fifth. There are two variations and they will work regardless if the key is Major or minor. Try it with the endings E.1 and E.2.

I --- IV7 --- diamond 10 m7 --- diamond 3⁷ --- diamond 8 m7 --- V11 --- I
OR   I7 --- IV7 --- diamond 10⁷--- diamond 3⁷---diamond 8 ⁷--- V11 --- I

Supplemental Information:

Minor key pieces, and there are many, seem to allow for an even greater selection of chords than those in Major keys, primarily because of movement into, and out of the relative major key.

SESSION 8 (A change of routine)
Songs that Modulate to Diamond 8
Reading Swing Rhythms

A.1) Read through the following bifid.

SESSION 8 Bifid

(No. 57)

A.2) Read through the following ballad.

SESSION 8 Ballad

(No. 58)

Four songs that temporarily modulate to diamond 8.

(Pick several keys and identify the Diamond 8 level of each. Verbally spell your tonic triad, and your diamond 8 chord.) The Roman numerals are related to the new temporary key. Here you arpeggiate in 8th notes, as is usual. All four of the following are in Ballad form, and the temporary modulation occupies much of the release/bridge. Therefore the given strophes are not the beginnings of the songs. You will keep in mind the home key that you choose, so that your apreggiation will be correct when you return to the home key.

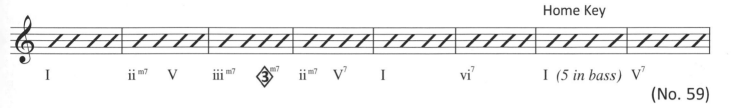

(No. 59)

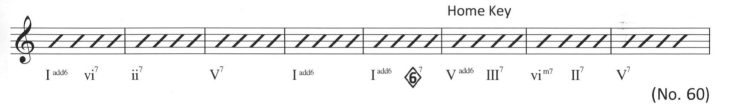

(No. 60)

(No. 61)

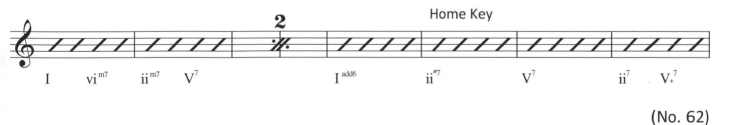

(No. 62)

Skill D: Sequences.

These two songs also modulate to Diamond 8. Again, the given strophes are not the beginnings of the songs, but rather the pertinent modulatory portions. Once again, remember the tonic chord of each particular home key.

D.1) Here is the second strophe of a song. Measures 3 and 4 (given here) should sequence 1 and 2. However, measures 7 and 8 should have free linear motion that seems to fit.

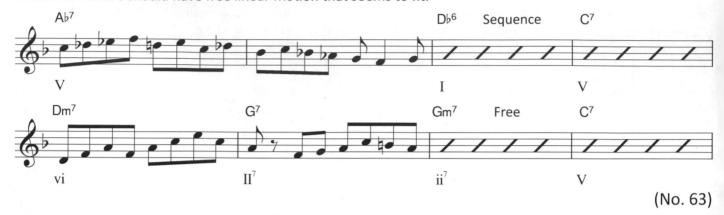

(No. 63)

D.2) Here is the release/bridge of another song. Measures 3 and 4 (given here) should sequence 1 and 2. And measures 7 and 8 should have free linear motion that seems to fit.

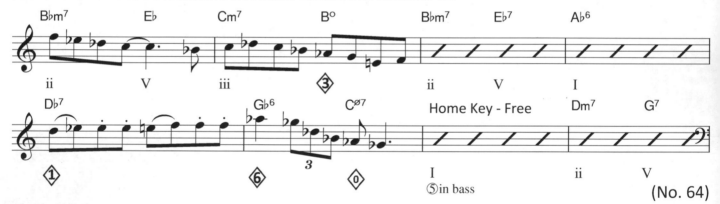

(No. 64)

Endings.

Another kind of ending, usually for slow songs, and involving a retard: On the last melodic note, put a substitute diamond I$_7$ perhaps with a fermata, that eventually resolves to a final I.

Supplemental Information: A Repetitive Blue-Note Hook.

Improvisation, while supposedly in a major key, can easily involve repeating an idea that dwells on either the low third scale degree, a subtonic, or even a low 5th scale degree. Appropriate neighbor notes, arrivals and resolutions make the musical idea all the more convincing. Notice the subsidiary notes in the following illustrations in the key of C. Pick a song and demonstrate this device.

SESSION 9
Reading Swing Rhythms

A.1) Read through the following bifid.

SESSION 9 Bifid

(No. 65)

A.2) Read through the following ballad.

SESSION 9 Ballad

(No. 66)

Four songs that temporarily modulate to diamond 3.

Pick several keys and identify the Diamond 3 level of each. Each time, verbally spell your tonic triad, and your diamond 3 chord. In the following strophes the Roman numerals are related to the temporary key. Here you arpeggiate in 8th notes, as is usual. The first two are the B sections of Bifids, and the second two are the release/bridge sections of Ballad forms. Keep in mind the home key that you choose, so that your arpeggiation will be correct when you return to the home key. Don't be thrown off by ③ of ③ .

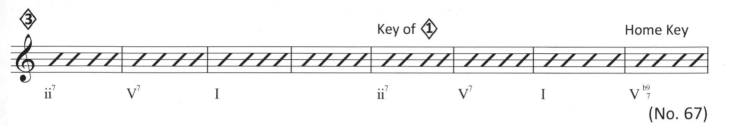

(No. 67)

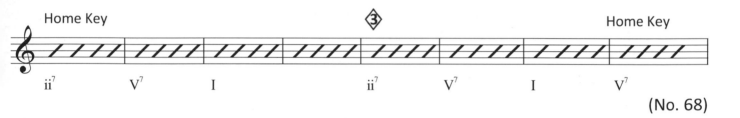

(No. 68)

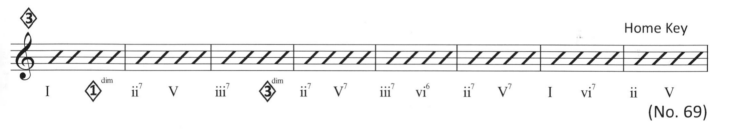

(No. 69)

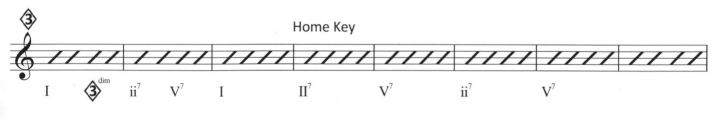

(No. 70)

Skill D: Response and Sequence.

The following 16 measures is the release/bridge of a ballad that also modulates to Diamond 3. It is a Ballad with double-length strophes (an occasional occurance). Put responses in measures 3-4 and 7-8. Sequence in measures 11-12 and 15-16.

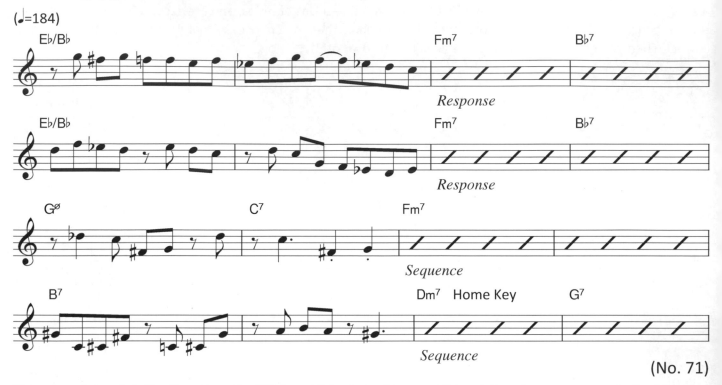

(No. 71)

This second stroph is the B section of a Bifid, and it is at the Diamond 3 level. Do a long sequence in the blank measures, while relating to the indicated chords.

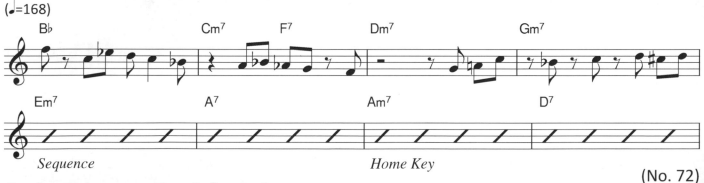

(No. 72)

Swing Versus Straight 8ths.

In listening to recordings of the great Jazz artists of the golden '50s, one notices that straight 8ths are sometimes intermingled with swing 8ths. The following is the bridge/release, and it passes through Diamond 3. Improvise a free line that follows the swing/straight directions.

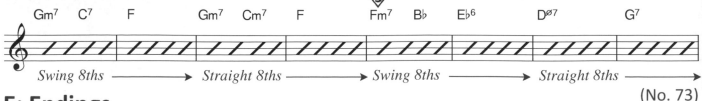

(No. 73)

E: Endings.

Sometimes an ending can fade while alternating between two chords in tempo. Here are some possibilities:
I --- v7, I^{M7}--- Diamond 10^{M7}, and i m7 --- IV^{Mm7}.

SESSION 10
1. A Little-Used Famous Progression.

There are at least five famous songs, the beginning of each with a variation on a chromatically descending chord progression. First decide on a key, then perform each in swing arpeggiation in a steady tempo. The teacher can serve as accompanist.

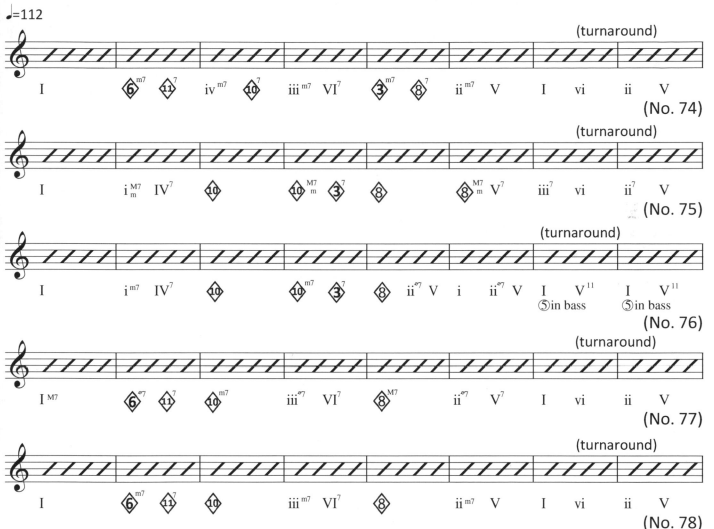

2. Hyper-Blues.

The twelve-bar blues are the first steps for beginners wanting to learn to play Jazz. Indeed, so much has been written and taught concerning Blues, that none of it will be repeated here. We are concerned with moving beyond basic Blues into a more rarified dimension.

Each of its basic chords can be enhanced by using polychords. The I triad can have a Diamond 6 Mm7 above it, the IV trial can have a Diamond 11 Mm7 above, and the V triad can have a Diamond 1 Mm7 above. Moreover, whoever is on the solo could stand to have a low-information (repetitive) riff softly accompanying them every four bars. Variety should be sought by either changing the riff, or by omitting riffs on various twelve bar strains. The sample here begins on the tonic note.

Example:

3. Half-Time Ideas During Super-Fast Jazz.

During very fast jazz pieces it is possible for some astonishing improvisers to ideate at the 8th note speed. (And more power to them!) An example would be the song "Cherokee" which is often done at break-neck speed. However, many good improvisers would justifiably prefer moving at the slower rate, proving that it is possible to satisfyingly ideate in a simultaneous quarter and half note rate of speed while the rhythm section maintains the faster rate. Perhaps Jazz listeners can more easily comprehend the slower rate, as well.

4. Ballad-Form Turnarounds (AABA).

A Turnaround is another name for a 1st ending. When the first A section ends, it is musically wrong to come to a musical close before repeating A all over again. Instead, chord formulas have come about that move smoothly into the repetition of A. The basic four chord formula is I --- vi --- ii --- V. Since Jazz invites chord substitutions, the following (and variants of them) are formulas that have proven their worth:

If the strophe ends on a melodic 1:
I --- Diamond 3^7 --- Diamond 8^7 --- V^{11}
IV^7--- Diamond 10^7 --- Diamond 3^7--- V^{11}

If the strophe ends on a melodic 3:
III^7--- VI^7--- II^7--- V^7

If the strophe ends on melodic 5:
iii^7 - Diamond 3^7 --- Diamond 8^{M7}--- V^7

Be on the alert for songs that have turnarounds already built into them.

E. Tag Ending Formulas.

An odd-seeming, but occasionally viable ending, especially for medium and faster speed pieces, is the SUDDEN FLURRY ENDING. In it, at a certain point, all players begin playing simultaneously fast random fragments/bits in order to create a controlled pandemonium. Then after the point has been made, all stop.

SESSION 11
1. Necessary Lower Information.

A major problem with improvisers is that their choruses have too much information. All too often audience members are expected to make sense of a chorus that is loaded with totally different ideas succeeding one another. The following is an illustration, albeit radically consistent, of how to lower information in choruses with the use of ideas that are then sequenced. Notice this is Ballad form, with the letters marked in the margins. Sometimes the sequence is two measures, and at other times four measures long. Read through the example in tempo. When breathing becomes necessary, feel free to omit some notes. (Jazz listeners are pretty smart, and will know what is implied.)

SEQUENCING
Ideas 1 measure long

(No. 79)

2. Roulades.

A roulade is a sudden spurt of fast notes. The use of them can add spice to any solo. Play this roulade in a tempo three or four times in a row.

3. Tollerance for Distorted Chords.

The chords accompanying improvising soloists should ideally be relatively clear. (See the first line of chords below.) However, it is possible that the soloist can play lines that are plainly outlining basic diatonic chords, while the accompanying harmony has, within limits, pleasing distortions. (Second line of chords.) The listener does not easily notice that the soloist is avoiding the chromatic notes in the harmony.

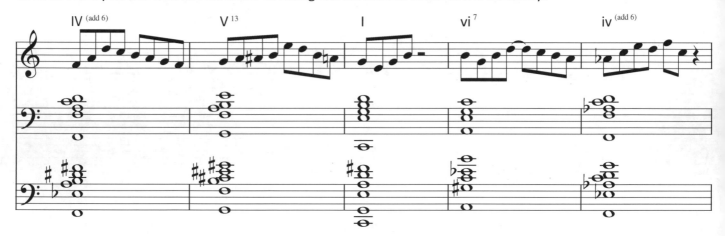

4. Vibrato Accents.

Read through the following in tempo, and hit the arrow notes with fast, and wide vibrato.

5. Overused Cliche Endings.

The following have been used so much that they seem devoid of any freshness.

SESSION 12
1. Consistent Two-Measure Sequences.

The following is in Ballad form, and you will be doing special things to the Bridge/Release. Read through it in tempo four times, each time with a different purpose or device.

1) The whole thing in swing rhythm, noticing the change of harmony in the Bridge/Release.
2) The whole thing, but with straight 8ths in measures 17-20.
3) The whole thing, but imitating a singer in quarter and half notes in measures 17-20.
4) The whole thing, but with a long held F (tonic note) in measure 17-18-19.

SEQUENCES
Ideas 2 measures long

(No. 80)

2. Benny Goodman-Type Rhythms.

Read through the following in tempo, noticing how the line makes the beat very obvious. As was said earlier, there are times when this effect is desirable.

(No. 81)

3. Rubato Rhythms.

The following strophe is written out in two ways: The first is with an uncomplicated 8th note feel, and works appropriately in the medium and fast speeds. Play it several times in tempo, trying out various medium and fast tempos.

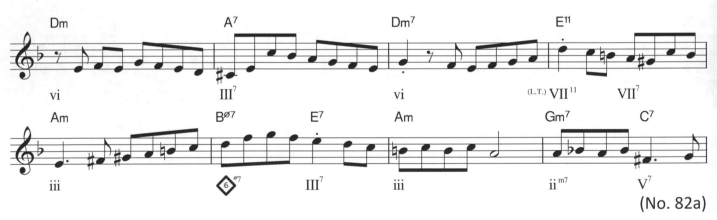

(No. 82a)

To play the above version in a slow tempo would be annoyingly tedious to the listener. What is more interesting is the same line played in rubato style during a steady beat. That way the line does not betray the beat, but rather "leans" on it. Pick a slow tempo and read through the following.

(No. 82b)

SESSION 13

1. Play a slow 1930s/'40s song from memory in the straightest possible rhythms.

2. Here are some old riffs put into a key/harmonic context. There are four examples to be done, each in its own key. Do all four in tempo exactly as they appear, and when you get to the last two measures, make up some balancing response that satisfactorily closes the thrice-heard riff. When improvising, it helps to occasionally use repeated riff passages. The listener relaxes in the familiarity.

Response

(No. 83)

Response

(No. 84)

Response

(No. 85)

Response

(No. 86)

45

3. Implied Polymeter.

The rhythmic effect of the first example goes back at least to the days of George Gershwin, and it implies that implied changing meter formula 3 + 3 + 2 that occupies two measures. The second example carries the concept even further (3 + 3 + 3 + 2).

4. Blue Notes.

Play the following, being careful to observe the repeat signs. This C major strophe demonstrates the three basic blue notes when plotted against a single major chord. The same relationship would be in effect on any other major triad.

5. Finding the 13th.

Listen to the string of V7 chords your teacher slowly plays, and find the 13th above the bass and play something that hovers around it until the chord changes.

6. Two-Speed Challenge.

Find a song that, from the accompaniment standpoint, moves in mainly half-notes (for example, "Cherokee"). Then improvise a chorus that simultaneously moves very rhythmically with an 8th-note feel.

SESSION 14
1. Filling Between Riffs.

Below are four self-contained strophes (I - IV - V - I), each in its own key and each has a repeating riff with holes that you will fill with changing bits. First play through each one as you see them. Then attempt filler. The filler you add should somehow aim at the next riff beginning. Don't be caught going the wrong way.

(No. 87)

(No. 88)

(No. 89)

(No. 90)

2. Vibrato Nudges.

First play the line as if there were no slurs. Then play the same line again and hold all the notes under the slur, bu[t] nudging each note with the use of vibrato. Notice the repeat sign.

♩=92

3. Certain Decorations.

Play the following line four times, each time adding the requested decoration on the second note in every measure.

First Reading: Add an on-the-beat 16th note that is a chromatic half step under the goal note.

Second: Add two on-th-beat 16th notes (an elevation) that start a diatonic third under the goal note.

Third: Add two on-the-beat 16th notes that chromatically surround the goal note.

Fourth: Add a relatively slow slide into the goal note.

Examples:

4. Song Grids.

Improvise a line in tempo that agrees with the harmony in the following two grids. The first is plain and the second is rare, but not so rare that it strays from the ii - V - I template. The first is a symmetric Bifid, and the second is asymmetric in length.

♩ = 144

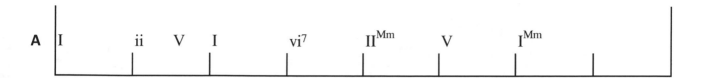

A | I — ii V I — vi⁷ — II^Mm — V — I^Mm — |

B | IV — I — ii⁷ — II^Mm — V |

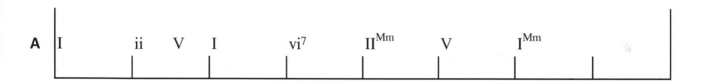

A | I — ii V I — vi⁷ — II^Mm — V — I^Mm — |

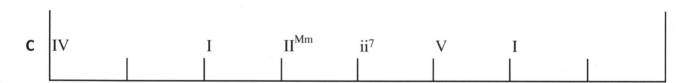

C | IV — I — II^Mm ii⁷ — V — I — |

(No. 91)

$\quad \downarrow = 72$

A | Cmm$^{7\,(M9)}$ | | | F^{13} | B$^{\flat 13}$ | E$^{\flat}$mm$^{7\,(M9)}$ | | | A$^{\flat 13}$ | D$^{\flat 13}$ |

B | C$^{\sharp}$m^{7} | E$^{\varnothing 7}$/F$^{\sharp}$ | Bm^{7} | | D$^{\varnothing 7}$/E | Am^{7} | | C$^{\varnothing 7}$/D | Gm^{7} | E$^{\flat 7\,(9)}$ | F$^{\varnothing 7}$/G |

A | Cmm$^{7\,(M9)}$ | | | F^{13} | B$^{\flat 13}$ | E$^{\flat}$mm$^{7\,(M9)}$ | A+/B | | A$^{\flat\varnothing 7}$/B$^{\flat}$ | E$^{\flat}$m $^{M7}_{M9}$ |

(No. 92)

50

SESSION 15
1. Growth by Step.

Improvising lines should often involve ideas that last for groups measures. One technique involves repeating, or seeming to repeat, the same idea, with one prominent pitch that continues growing by step in the same direction, usually upward. The following illustration certainly seems obvious, but it is intended to make the above point. Where you see arrows, play a series of pitches that continue to grow up by step. The growth would be scalar 5 - 6 - 7 - 8. Notice the different keys. Aside from the step-growth, don't fail to notice how much is exactly repeated (only three times), and how monotony is still avoided with the growth component. Here are two examples. Play them, filling in the arrow notes, as directed.

2. Very Slow Swing and that Third Beat Partial.

The following has been written out accurately in the compound meter that is the swing feeling. In an assiduously steady beat (dotted quarter note = 120), play the melody with a slightly louder dynamic on the tenuto notes. For the authentic swing feeling this is a technique to be used not only in slow, but also in somewhat faster tempos.

3. The Idea That Rises by Minor Thirds.

Play through the two examples below, and notice how the same two beat idea rises, and falls by minor thirds. Try the same thing with the given three examples. Maybe the accompanying harmony should be a single triad throughout, and maybe such a technique should be only occasionally used for shock/coloristic value.

4. Song Grids.

Improvise choruses on the following two harmonic grids, one plain, and the other rare. The meter is 4/4, and, as before, each grid square is worth four beats. Later, pick one of the grids and improvise a 3/4 chorus. Because it is in triple meter, each grid square should then last two measures.

♩ = 152

$II^7 = II^{Mm}$

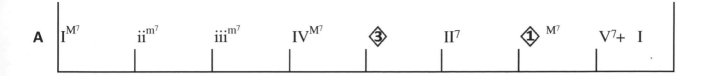

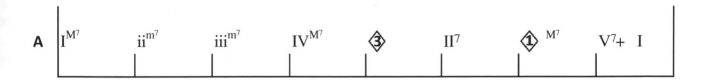

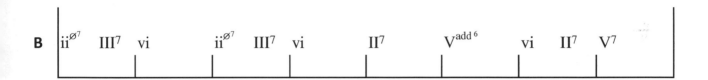

(No. 93)

(No. 94)

SESSION 16
1. Basic Counterlines.

When some other instrument is playing a melody (the Head), basic counterlines of little musical interest can serve as accompaniment. They should attract little attention so as not to upstage the main melody. And they should generally stay away from the area of the melody to avoid unwanted collisions. Below are two examples. The first is a Bifid-form with the second strophe in the Diamond 3 key. It has harmony changing every measure, hence the speed of the counterline. The second is a Ballad-form and has a counterline to match the faster harmonic change. Both show where the BREAK is, and thus those notes, instead of holding, would abruptly break off.

(No. 95)

(No. 96)

55

2. More on Polymeter (continued from Session 13).

Though the meter is of course 4/4, ongoing 8th notes can imply a brief simultaneous feeling of 3/8. Whatever the simultaneous underpinning harmony is, and it should remain in 4/4, this line would seem to temporarily break with it. Numbers 3 and 4 are especially dissonant against the harmony. Here is another technique that, once again, should only be occasionally used for shockcoloristic value. Such brief dissonant jaunts can easily jolt the casual listener expecting the ordinary.

4. Song Grids.

Improvise choruses on the two following progressions, one plain, the other rare. Notice how slowly the chords change in the rare one.

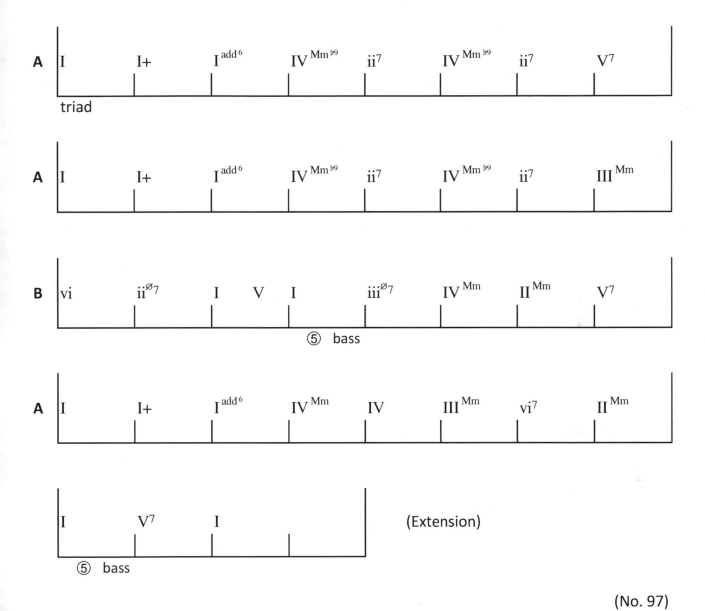

(No. 97)

♩= 176

A Cm^7 | | D^7 | | $G^{7(\flat 9)}$ | | $C^{7(\flat 9)}$ |

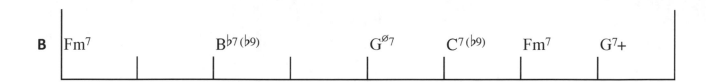

B Fm^7 | | $B^{\flat 7(\flat 9)}$ | | $G^{\varnothing 7}$ | $C^{7(\flat 9)}$ | Fm^7 | G^7+ |

A Cm^7 | | D^7 | | $D^{\varnothing 7}$ | $G^{7(\flat 9)}$ | $C^{7(\flat 9)}$ |

C $A^{\varnothing 7}$ | $A^{\flat}m^{(M7)}$ | Gm^7 | $C^{7(\flat 9)}$ | Fm^7 | $B^{\flat 13}$ | $E^{\flat (add\,6)}$ |

(No. 98)

4. Penultimate Chorus Sample

The written-out penultimate chorus for several simultaneous performers: After all the improvisation choruses are finished, and before the Head is replayed, it can be satisfying to hear a number of players simultaneously playing a pre-planned variation in improvisational style. The following is just such an example. Read through it in strict tempo.

(No. 96)

SESSION 17
Emphasis on Harmony, using Frozen Chord Structures

For this session you will be at the piano. In pencil, re-spell the given chord in the succeeding measures, calculating up from the given bass notes. In the two blank measures, decide on your own bass note on which to build the chord. Be prepared to then play your strophe of chords.

Number 4 is colored by the internal stacking of perfect 4ths. Number 9 is colored by the clustered notes. The resolution notes in 7 and 8 do not have to take place. Numbers 1 through 4 can be used on I's and IV's. Numbers 5 through 9 can be used on V's and IV's. Number 10 is used on ii's. Numbers 11 and 12 are vague and can be used when that quality is wanted.

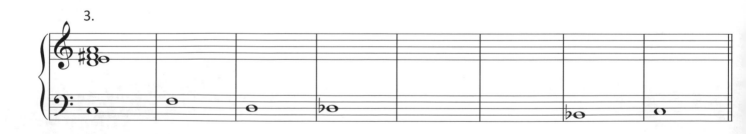

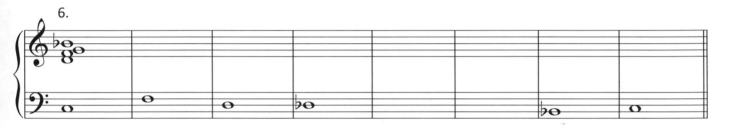

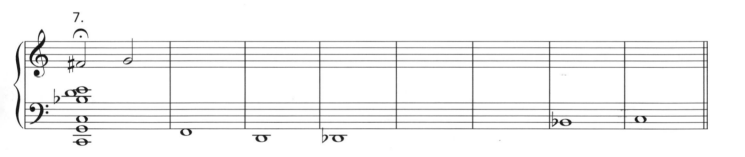

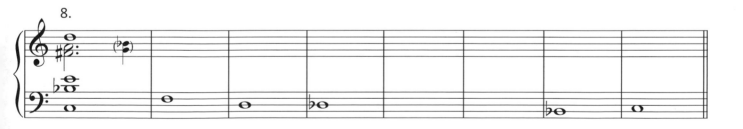

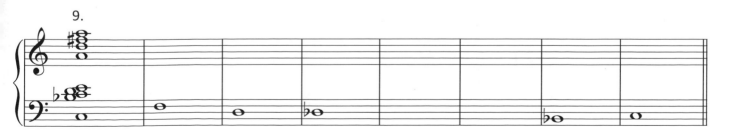

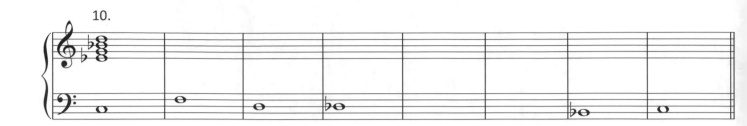

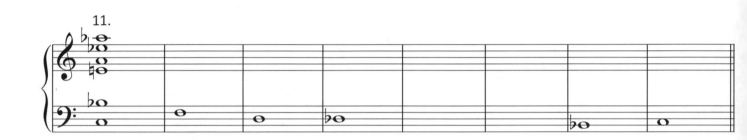

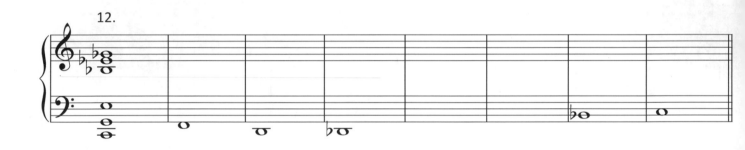

SESSION 18
1. Classic Overall Form for Jazz Song Presentation.

First the song is played plainly, then the improvisatory variations (any number of players and variations), then, (possibly) when planned and written out, a penultimate unison variation, followed by the final appearance of the song played 70% plainly. (The implication being that the song has been affected by the variations, but it still has to be recognizable at this point.)

2. Links.

Play the following strophe twice, and both times when you get to the last two measures, where the melody seems to stop "to get its breath," improvise a link that is in mostly 8th notes that leads to the beginning, or to a hypothetical next strophe.

Link

3. Paired Doubling.

Listen to the given strophe, and then upon hearing it again and while staying in the key, try to double it a third under. Then do it all a second time, doubling the melody a sixth under. Then do it a third time, using 3rds for a while, and 6ths at other times.

4. Equal Intervals in Lines.

For the occasional step outside tonality: Play the following in strict tempo.

5. Copycat.

The teacher will play all of the following, one at a time, in tempo. But you won't know which one the teacher will choose. First you hear a measure, and you immediately immitate it in the next. Continue that process until all eight examples have been done. After that has been done, do all eight again (out of order), but this time play responses to what you have heard.

6. A Sample Filigree Unison Chorus.

Read through the following (on page 65) in tempo.

Penultimate Chorus Sample

♩ = 160

(No. 100)

SESSION 19
1. Paraphrase Pieces.

"In a Mellow Tone" is a paraphrase of the song "Rose Room." More simply put, the chord changes of "Rose Room" were used to create the melody of "In a Mellow Tone." "Groovin' High" likewise uses the changes of "Whispering." There are certainly more examples. Can you think of any?

2. Caressing the Chords.

Since the playing of Jazz involves playing by ear, a good experience would be for the teacher to hold certain chords, having four or five discrete pitches spaced in 3rds and 4ths. Then, with no tempo, play so that you move by step in and out of the chord, perhaps in groups of notes that for a while move in the same melodic direction.

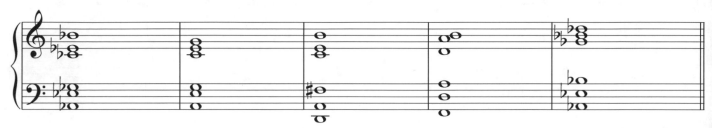

3. Fast, Wide and/or Accelerating Vibrato Accents.

Play the following example in tempo, and play the arrow notes with obvious vibrato accents. This challenge serves as an excuse to point out that the most acclaimed jazz artists of the golden era employed vibrato, every throb of which was conveying jazz rhythms.

4. Hearing the ii - V - I and "Feeling Your Way Around by Ear."

Notice the given chords. You will be playing them at the piano. The following involves a melody (on the next page) of a simulated 1920 - 1960 popular song that will be slowly played by the teacher. After reading the directions, you will play the appropriate chords as the melody transpires. Some chords may last a measure, while others change half-way through. Watch out for the modulation to Diamond 3 in two measures.

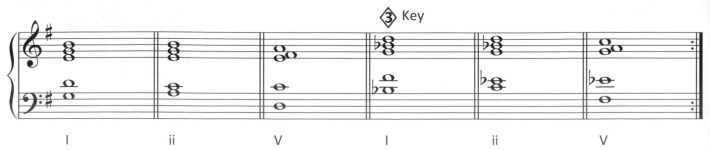

Here is the melody for the previous chord progression.

4. Spurts of Sixteenth Notes.

In a moderate tempo piece, most of the action is in 8th notes, with occasional articulation rests. Players often keep their listeners' attention with occasional, unexpected very loud single notes, as well as with spurts of constant 16th notes in two to four measures length. In the following challenge you are to improvise a line mostly in 8ths, except that you choose perhaps two inner measures to break into scale-like 16ths. Then resume the 8th note motion.

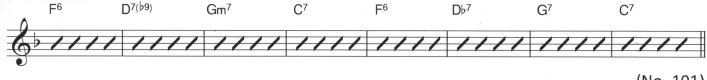

(No. 101)

5. The Haunting Melody.

Jazz players, being mental song collectors, are so sensitive that they latch on to melodies that haunt them. Have you ever thought in this way, and could you name two such songs? For some the following two would qualify: Kurt Weill's "Here I'll Stay," and Ralph Rainger's "If I Should Lose You."

6. Staffless Contour Lines and Changeable Chord Grids.

The grids on the following page have no staff, but do convey note lengths, rests, and generalized contours (when the line goes up, and when it goes down). Using the given contour and rhythms, in tempo, adapt your improvised line to the changing harmony of two different harmonic grids.

7. Another Penultimate Chorus.

Play through the sample in tempo on pages 69-70.

E. Two Types of Endings.

An ending that might occasionally be used for slower tempo pieces is the ritard and the fermata on the last chord. And like any formula, if used too often it can be annoying.

Occasionally abrupt endings add variety to a set. While this can be used at the very end of tags, it is probably most pleasingly shocking when there is no tag.

(No. 102)

(No. 103)

Penultimate Chorus Sample

(No. 104)

ADDENDUM A

(for accompanying C instruments)

No. 1

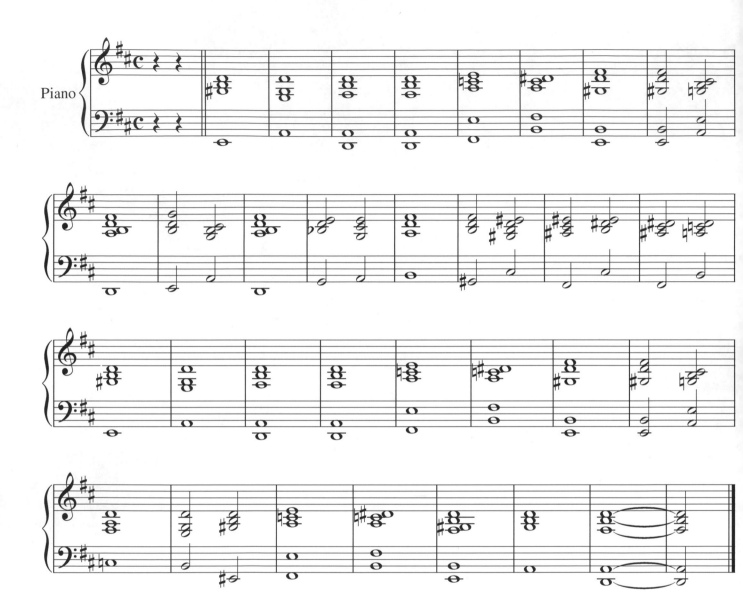

No. 2

First Session
No. 3 - 8

No. 9

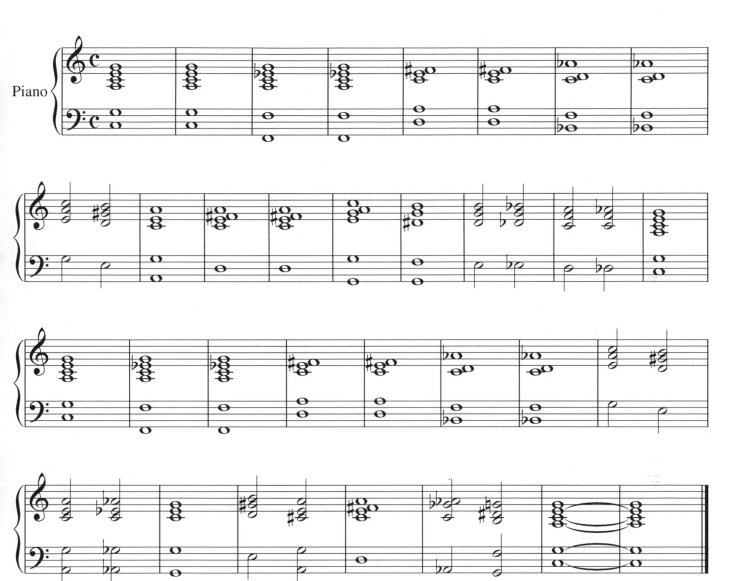

No. 10

Second Session
No. 11 - 16

No. 17

No. 18

Third Session
No. 19 - 24

No. 25

No. 26

Fourth Session
No. 27 - 32

No. 33

No. 34

Fifth Session
No. 35 - 40

No. 41

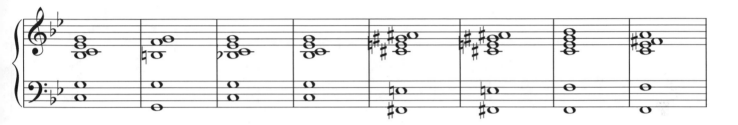

No. 42

Sixth Session
No. 43 - 48

No. 49

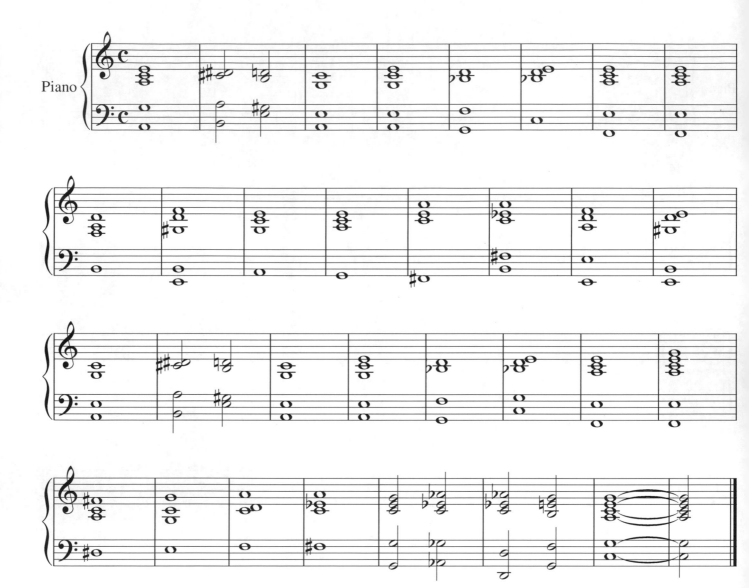

No. 50

Piano

Seventh Session
No. 51 - 56

No. 57

No. 50

Eighth Session
No. 59 - 64

Possible Keys

95

No. 65

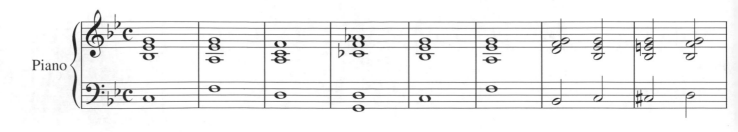

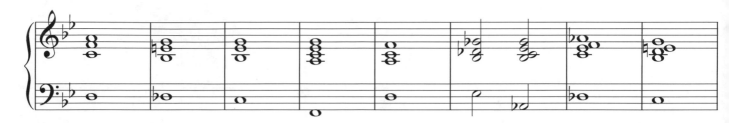

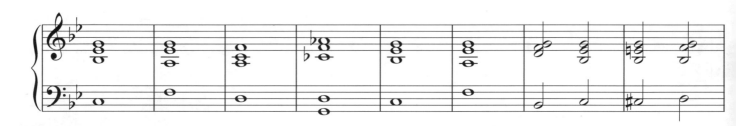

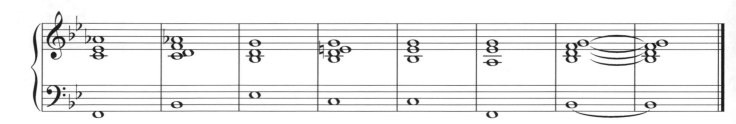

No. 66

Ninth Session
No. 67 - 69

Default keys

67. Diamond 3   Diamond 1   Home Key

Piano

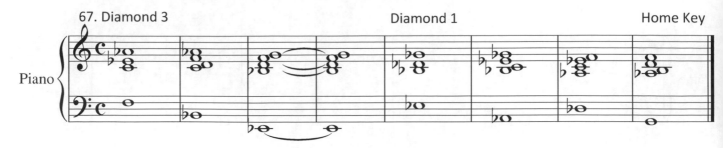

68. Home Key   Diamond 3   Home Key

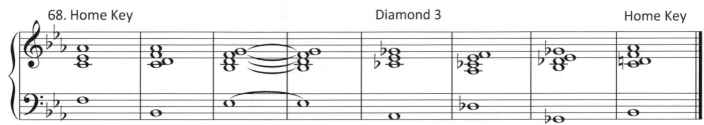

69. Diamond 3

Home Key

98

No. 70 - 73

No. 74 - 78

Eleventh and Twelfth Sessions
No. 79/80

Twelfth and Thirteenth Sessions
No. 81 - 86

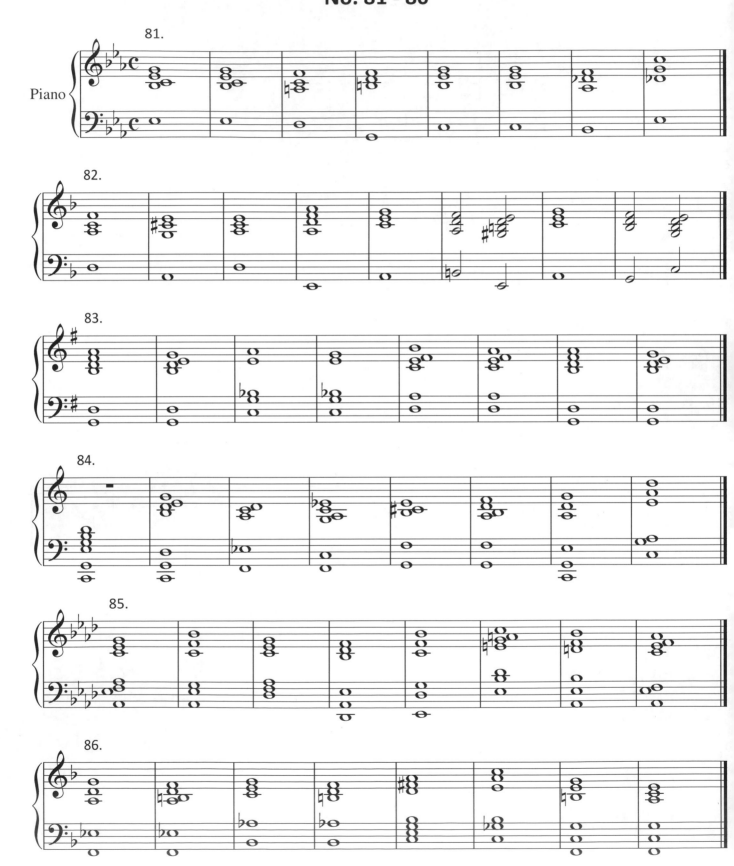

Piano

Fourteenth Session
No. 87 - 90

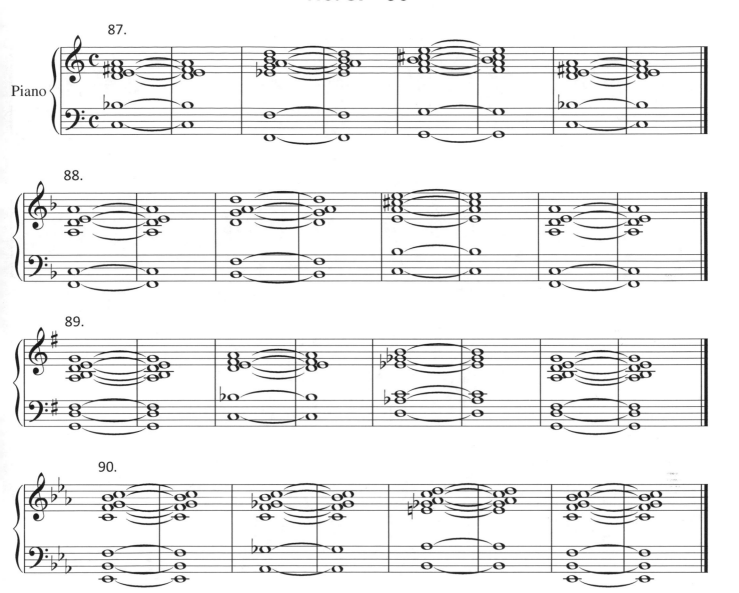

No. 91

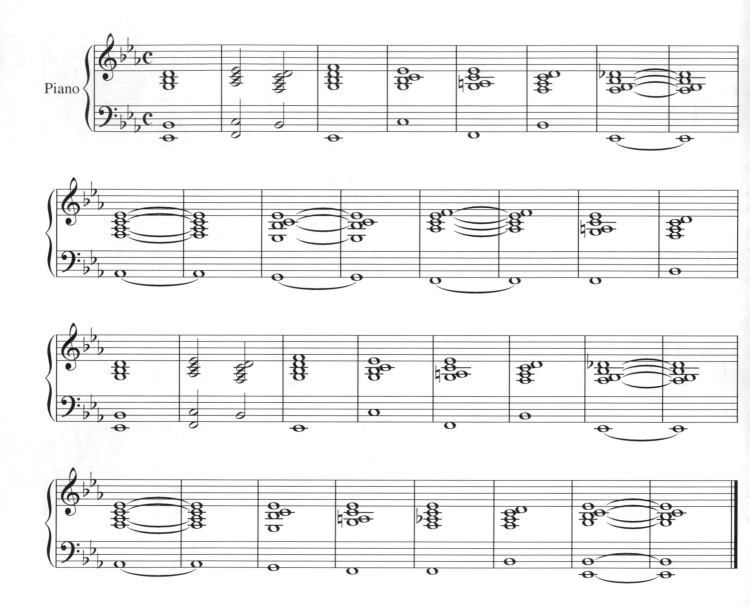

No. 92

No. 93

Piano

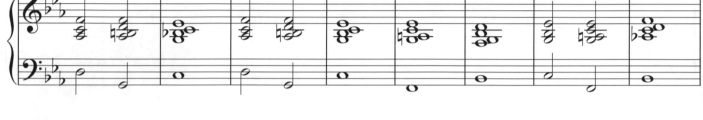

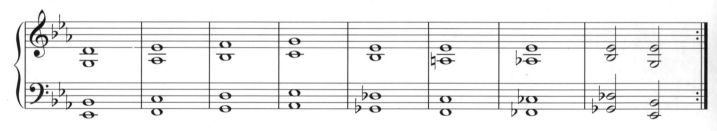

No. 94

No. 95

No. 96

No. 97

No. 98

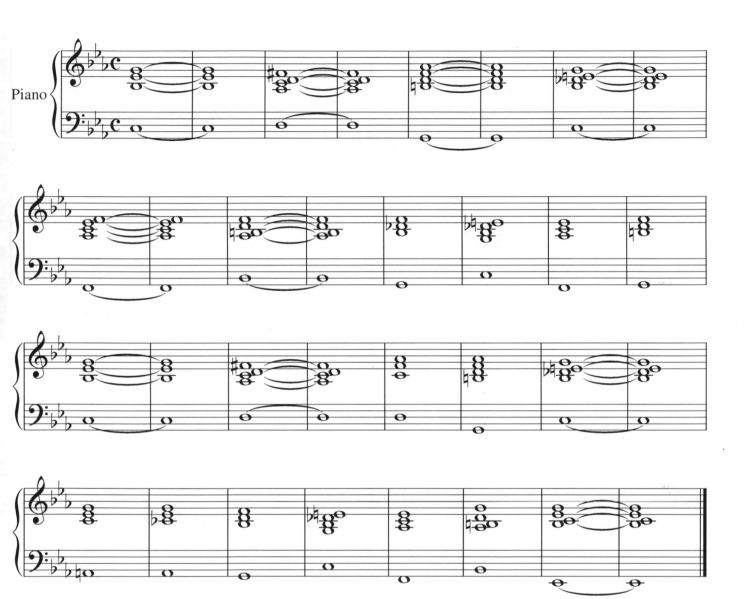

No. 99

No. 100

No. 101 - 103

No. 104

ADDENDUM B

(for accompanying B-flat instruments)

No. 1

No. 2

First Session
No. 3 - 8

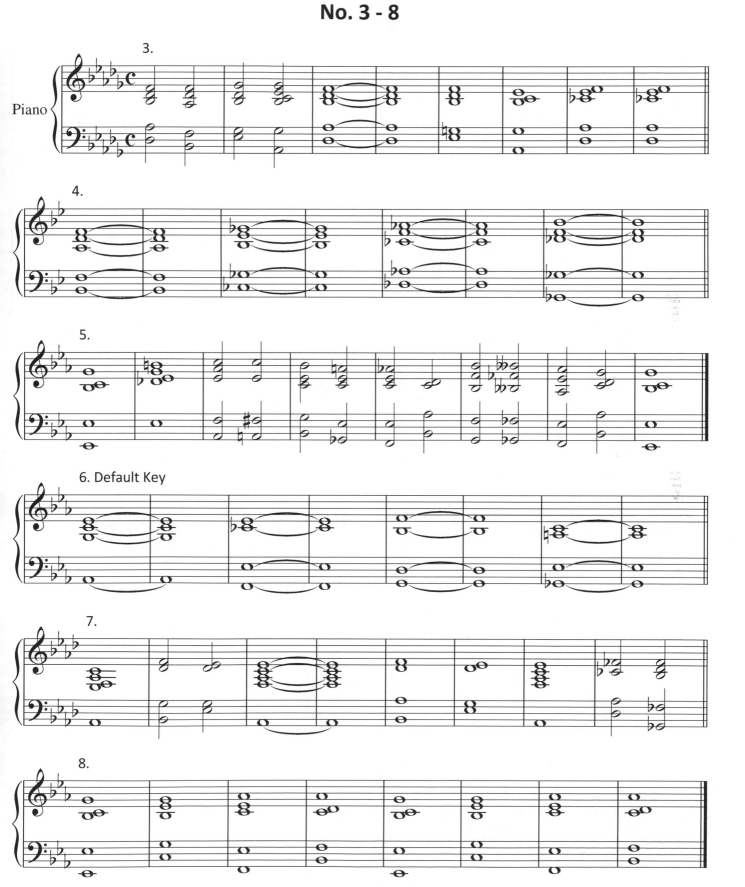

No. 9

No. 10

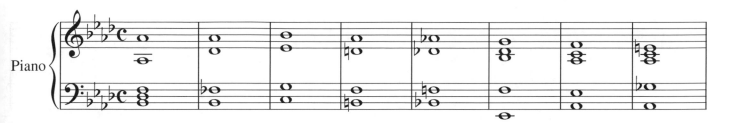

Second Session
No. 11 - 16

No. 17

No. 18

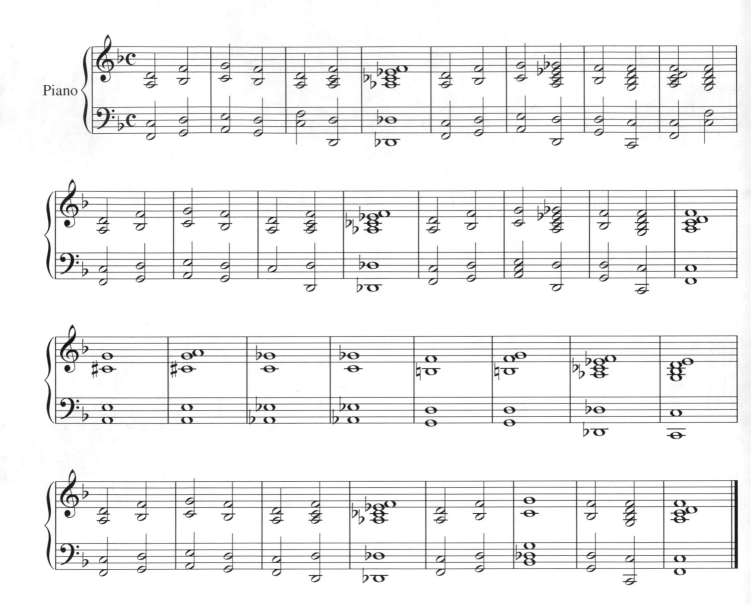

Third Session
No. 19 - 24

No. 25

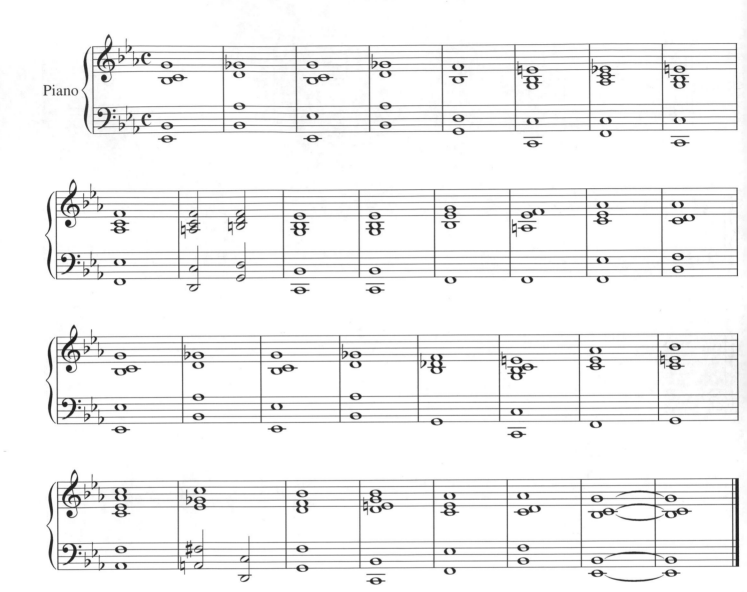

No. 26

Piano

Fourth Session
No. 27 - 32

128

No. 33

No. 34

Fifth Session
No. 35 - 40

No. 41

No. 42

Sixth Session
No. 43 - 48

No. 49

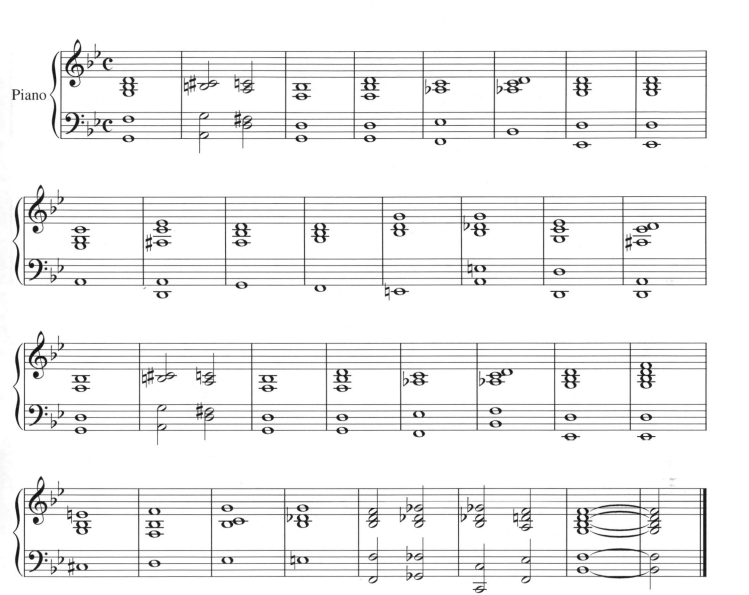

No. 50

Seventh Session
No. 51 - 56

No. 57

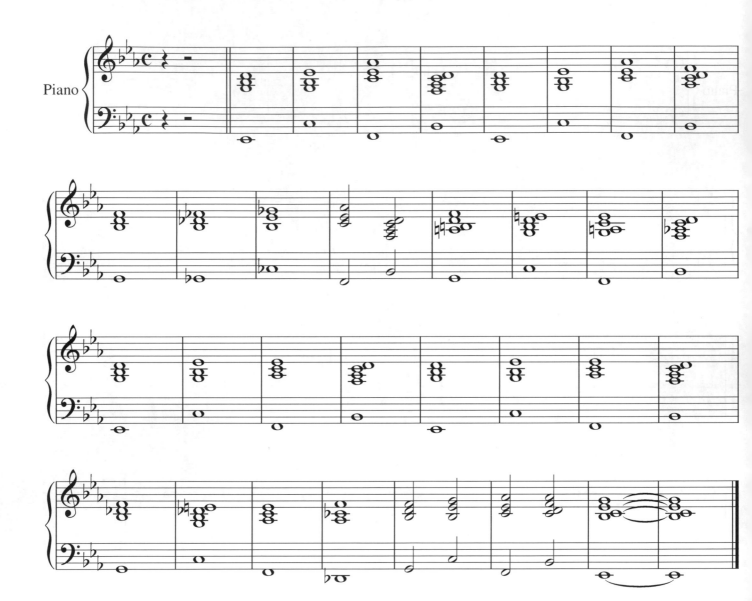

No. 50

Eighth Session
No. 59 - 64

No. 65

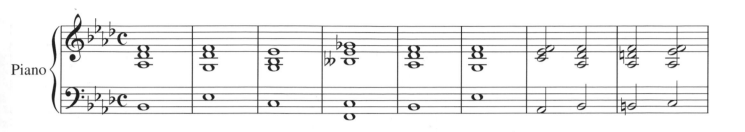

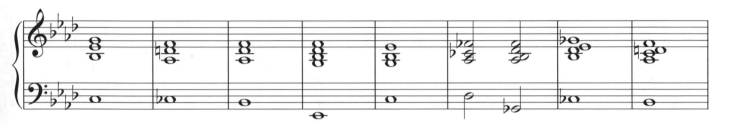

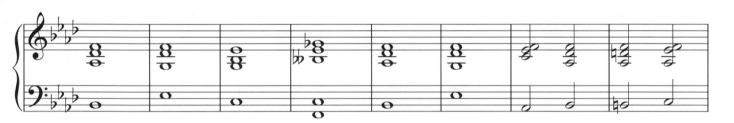

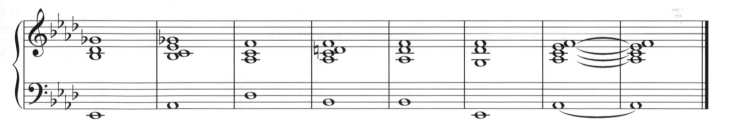

No. 66

Ninth Session
No. 67 - 69

Default keys

No. 70 - 73

No. 74 - 78

Eleventh and Twelfth Sessions
No. 79/80

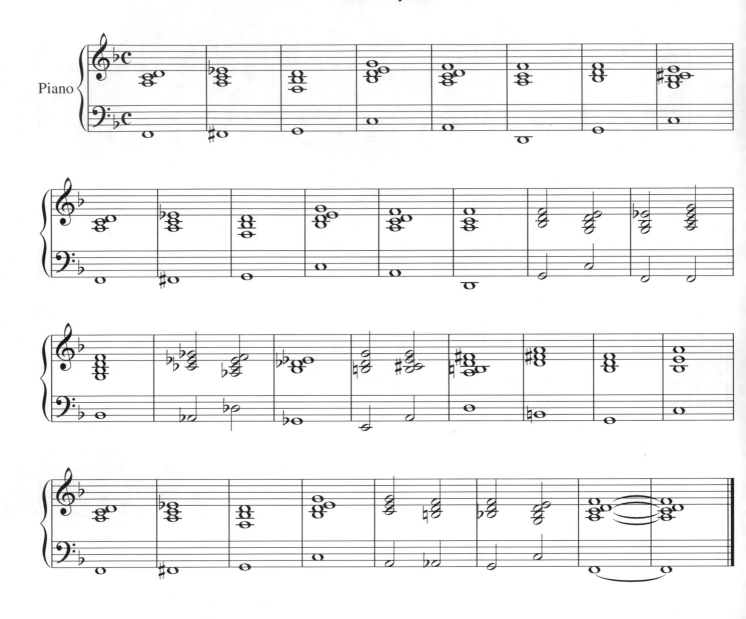

Twelfth and Thirteenth Sessions
No. 81 - 86

Piano

Fourteenth Session
No. 87 - 90

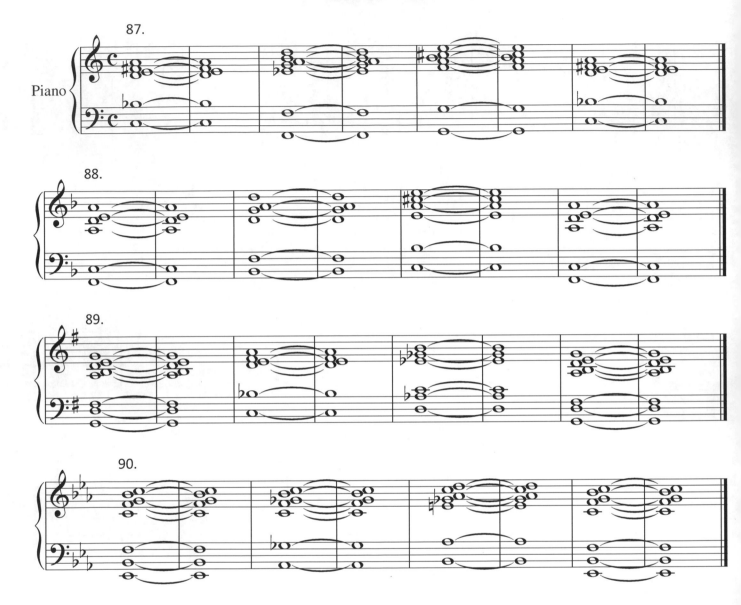

No. 91

No. 93

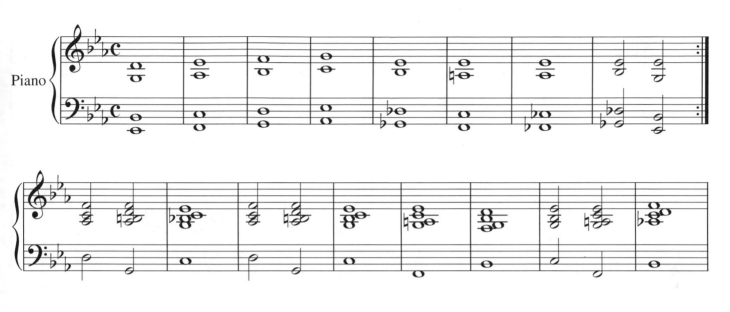

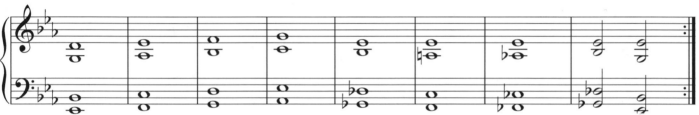

No. 94

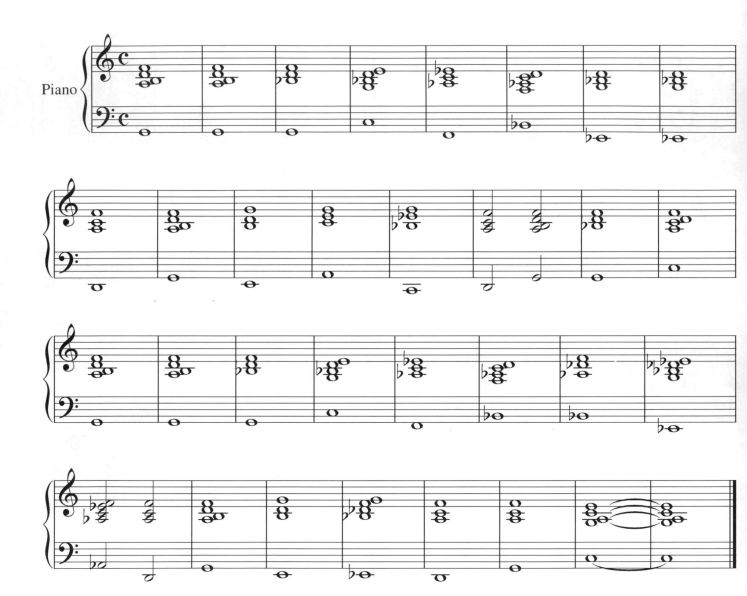

No. 95

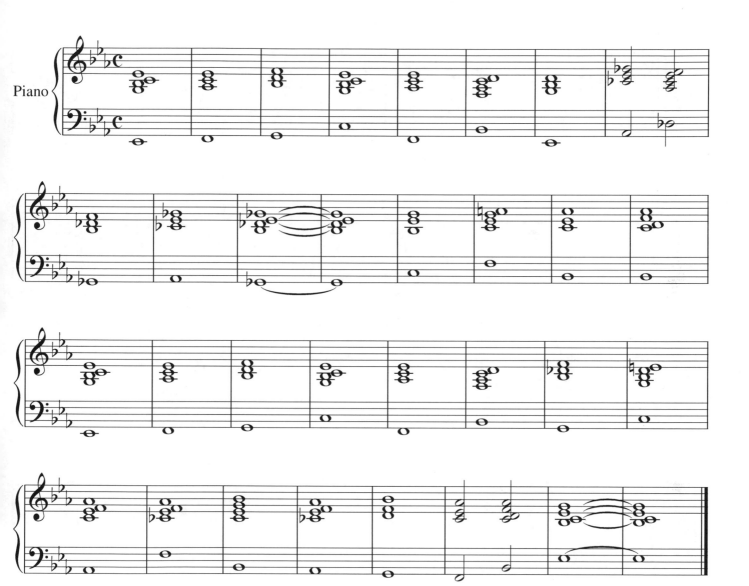

No. 96

No. 97

No. 98

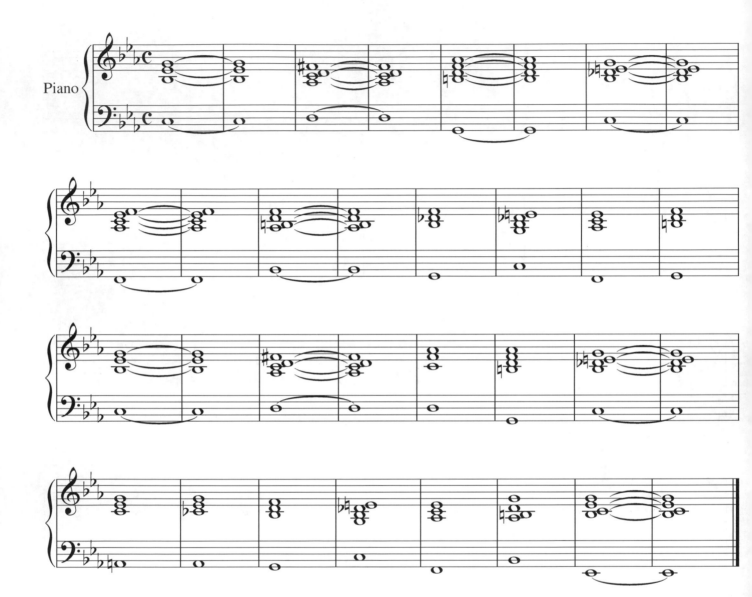

No. 99

No. 100

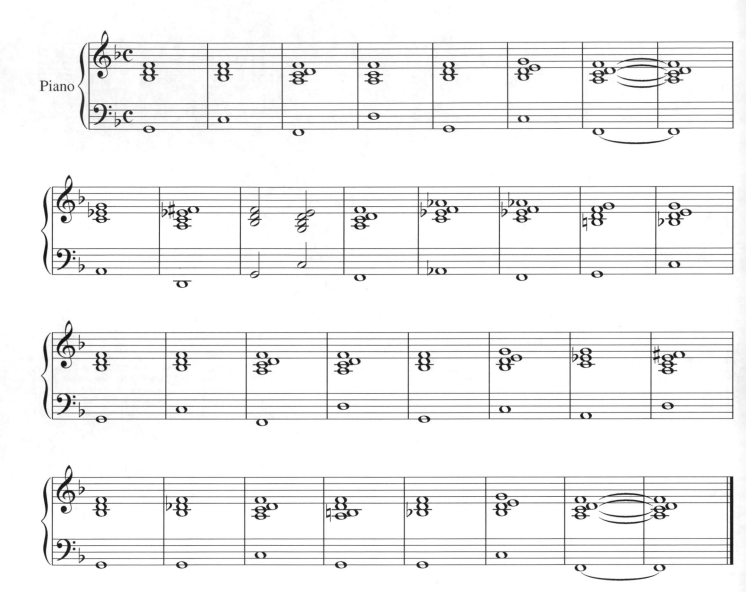

No. 101 - 103

No. 104

ADDENDUM C

(for accompanying E-flat instruments)

No. 1

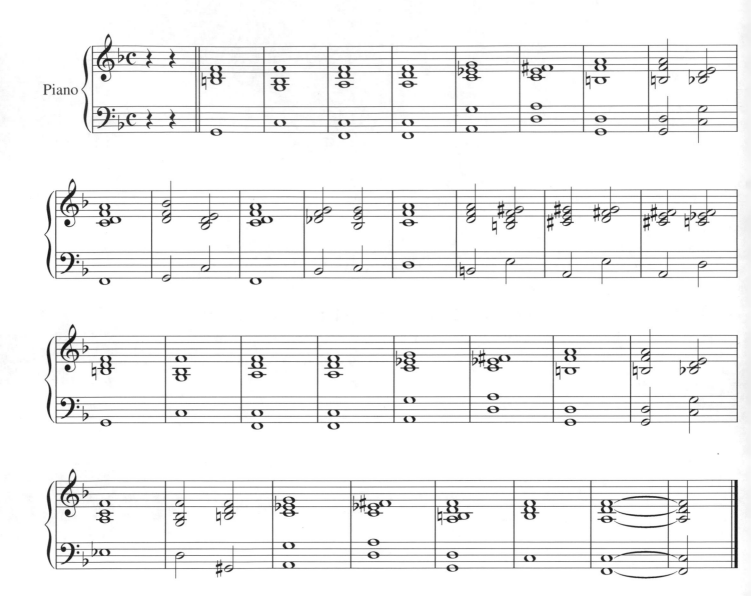

No. 2

First Session
No. 3 - 8

No. 9

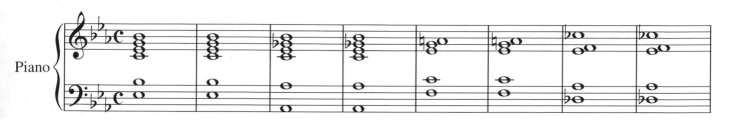

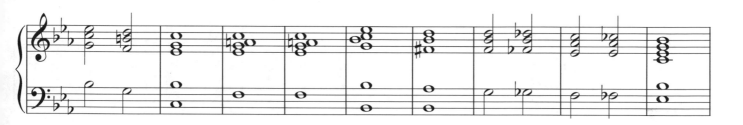

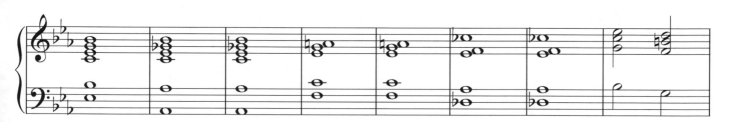

No. 10

Second Session
No. 11 - 16

No. 17

Piano

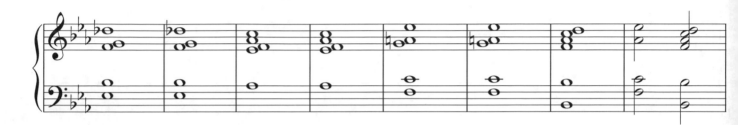

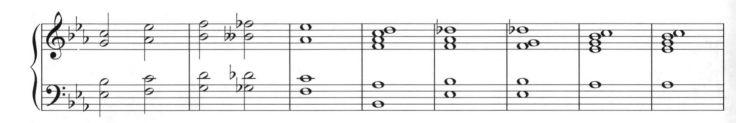

No. 18

Third Session
No. 19 - 24

No. 25

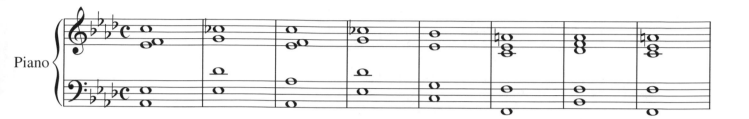

No. 26

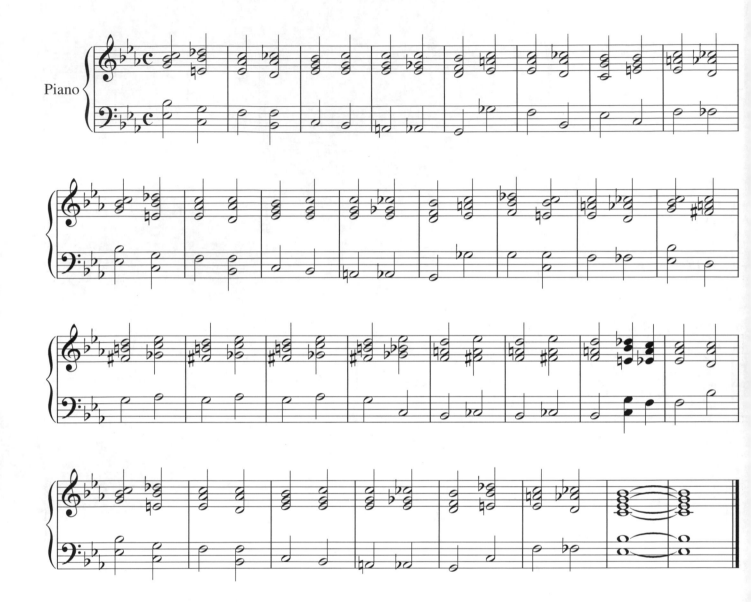

Fourth Session
No. 27 - 32

No. 33

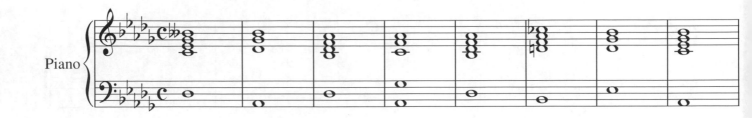

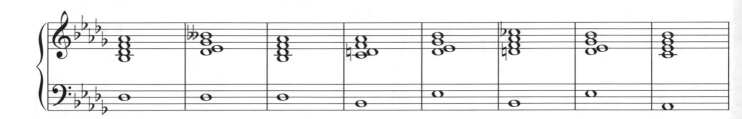

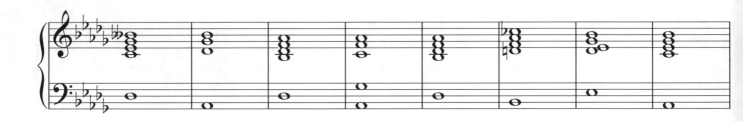

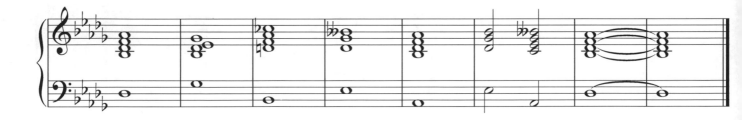

No. 34

Fifth Session
No. 35 - 40

No. 41

No. 42

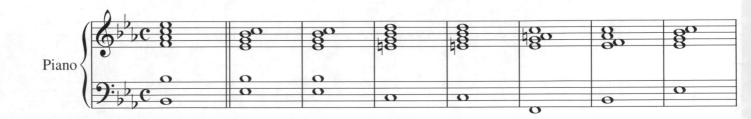

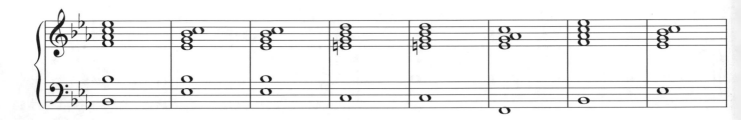

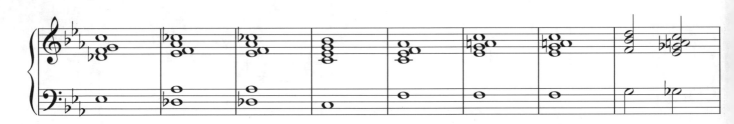

Sixth Session
No. 43 - 48

No. 49

No. 50

Piano

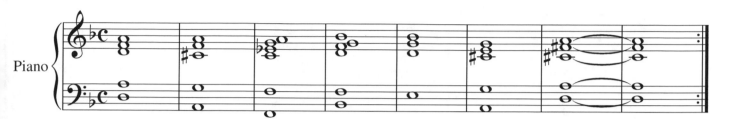

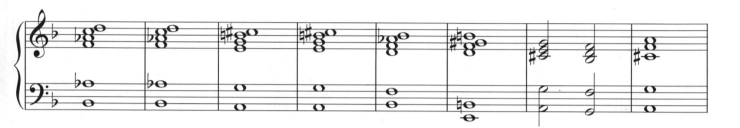

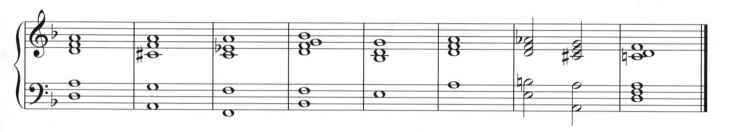

Seventh Session
No. 51 - 56

No. 57

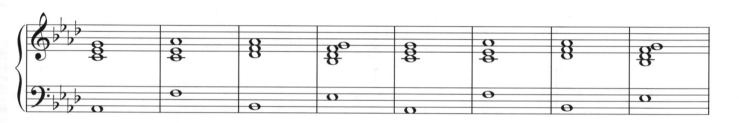

No. 50

Piano

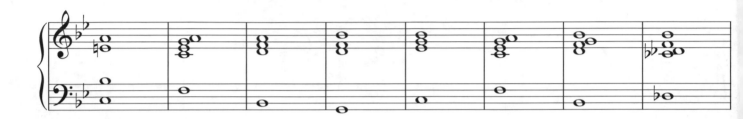

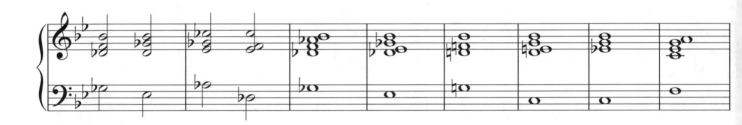

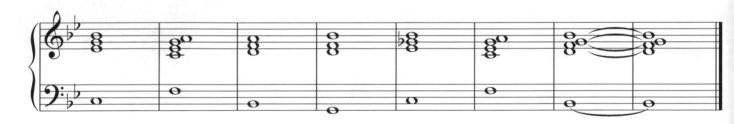

Eighth Session
No. 59 - 64

No. 65

No. 66

Ninth Session
No. 67 - 69

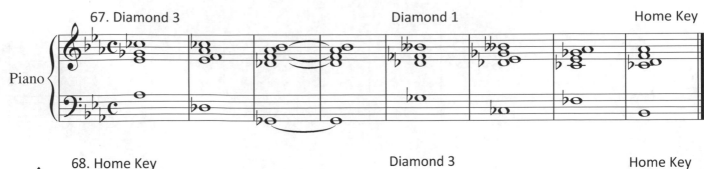

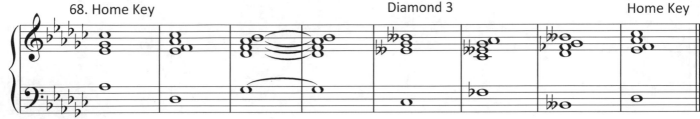

No. 70 - 73

189

No. 74 - 78

Eleventh and Twelfth Sessions
No. 79/80

191

Twelfth and Thirteenth Sessions
No. 81 - 86

Fourteenth Session
No. 87 - 90

Piano

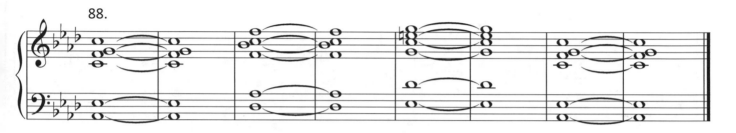

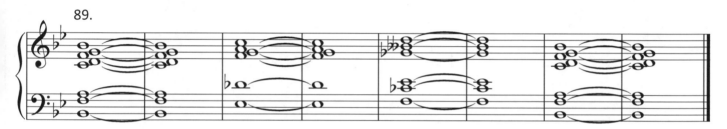

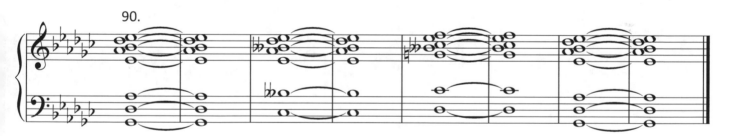

No. 91

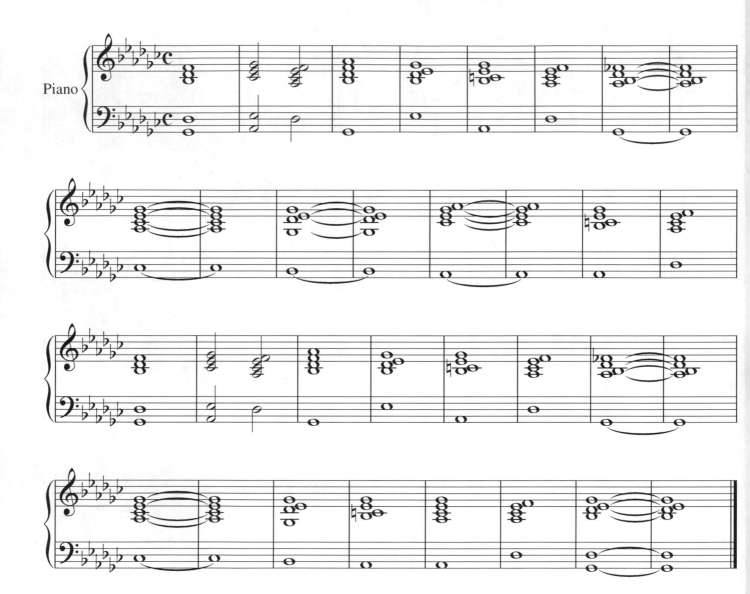

No. 92

No. 93

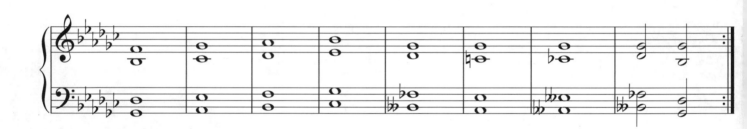

No. 94

No. 95

Piano

No. 96

No. 97

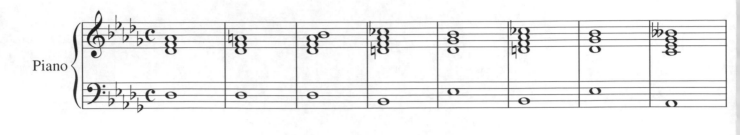

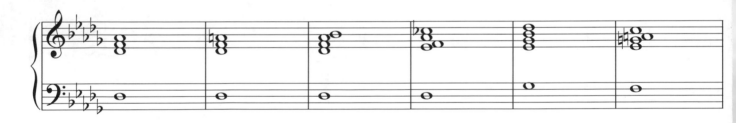

No. 98

No. 99

No. 100

No. 104